Celebrating
AROUND THE Table

Trillia J. Newbell

HARVEST HOUSE PUBLISHERS
EUGENE, OREGON

Published in association with Don Gates of the literary agency The Gates Group, www.the-gates-group.com

Photography by Jay Eads
Illustrations by Stephen Crotts
Cover design by Faceout Studio, Elisha Zepeda
Interior design by Faceout Studio, Paul Nielsen
Pattern artwork (cover and interior) © RODINA OLENA / Shutterstock

Celebrating Around the Table

Text copyright © 2024 by Trillia Newbell
Artwork copyright © 2024 by Stephen Crotts
Published by Harvest House Publishers
Eugene, Oregon 97408
www.harvesthousepublishers.com

ISBN 978-0-7369-8896-4 (hardcover)
ISBN 978-0-7369-8897-1 (eBook)

Library of Congress Control Number: 2023951953

Printed in China

24 25 26 27 28 29 30 31 32 / RDS—FO / 10 9 8 7 6 5 4 3 2 1

To my dad, mom, sisters, husband, and kids:
You have shaped, loved, served, and cared for me.

And to the men and women who have gone before us
to make it all possible.

Contents

Welcome 9

WEEK ONE Freedom

Frederick Douglass 23
Elizabeth Freeman 35
Harriet Tubman 43
Recipes 55

WEEK TWO Mission

Betsey Stockton 71
George Liele 81
Charlotte L. Forten Grimké 89
Recipes 99

WEEK THREE Guide

Lemuel Haynes 115
Ruby Bridges 125
John Perkins 133
Recipes 143

WEEK FOUR Messenger

Phillis Wheatley 157
Sojourner Truth 167
Mahalia Jackson 177
Recipes 187

Continuing to Celebrate 199
Notes 202
Recipe Index 207

Welcome

If you are familiar with my work, you'll know that I have a desire to provide a refreshing narrative to our conversations regarding race and ethnicity. In short, I desire for us to do more delighting, celebrating, and enjoying our differences. One way that I've personally embraced celebration is through my family's intentional approach to observing Black History Month.

Although we observe Black History Month during February, these exercises have spilled out into other months and various cultures and people groups. We've learned about others from Australia, Africa, and Asia. Every February, I post about our family's journey of learning and celebrating, and each year, people ask to join in. *Celebrating Around the Table* is my invitation for you to join us!

Before I get into the details, let's consider why we should learn about Black history. Getting to know our shared past throughout the year can help us gain understanding and perspective. Specifically, in the church, it can be a means of building community and helping us learn how to bear one another's burdens (Galatians 6:2). Bearing the burden of another is a way to love our neighbor as ourselves (Matthew 22:39). Our nation's history of oppression and segregation continues to carry a sting for many, both white and Black. Understanding the gravity of all that has happened can only help us in relating to the pain so many still carry.

A knowledge and understanding of others' history can be a catalyst for open dialogue. Of course, we wouldn't want to assume that knowledge equates to full understanding, but it can help. Furthermore, and possibly most importantly, this knowledge can inspire a genuine interest in others (when done as unto the Lord). This will lead to opportunities to share the gospel and mutual fellowship.

In 1976, the United States government officially designated February as Black History Month, an annual, monthlong celebration of noted Black historians, scholars, educators, publishers, and others here in America. For me, school days during the month of February meant learning about historical Black figures like Frederick Douglass, Rosa Parks, and Martin Luther King Jr.

The posters would go up and we'd be required to dive in and do heavy research on who these people were and what they did. But as quickly as the posters went up, they disappeared when the calendar turned over to March 1. As earnest as our research had been, once February ended, these people were basically forgotten.

February is a wonderful time to reflect on the lives of Black Americans and the contributions they had on society. It's a time to teach kids about a key aspect of American history. One motto I repeat a lot is "Either we will teach our children, or the culture will." Parents ask me frequently, "Where do I begin?" This book provides a place to start as you explore our shared history, open the door for questions from your children, consider how to think from a biblical worldview, and celebrate our differences. My hope in providing you with this resource is to give you a place to start. But I also hope that you'll pull out this book in July and October. As you get a small taste of the stories featured here, I hope you'll want to do more digging for yourself. You don't have to wait until February to learn about the lives of Black people in our culture. You can do it all year long!

Here's how *Celebrating Around the Table* works. Each week will include three celebration experiences along with the following:

- ❋ Recipes for you to use featuring traditional Black dishes inspired by history or my momma's kitchen.
- ❋ A brief biographical sketch of a historical Black Christian with commentary from me and samples of their work, where possible.
- ❋ A devotional reflection based on an aspect of the person's life or a lesson from the story, such as seeing the image of God in others, courage in tough situations, how the gospel frees us from the slavery of sin, and more.

* Discussion Questions: These provide opportunities for you and your family or friends to dig deeper and apply what you are learning.
* Kids' Corner Question: A special question for you to use if you are discussing the content with children.
* A prayer prompt based on the theme and devotional to help you go to the Lord, who loves to hear us.

Each week has a theme to help guide your readings and discussions. The themes highlight an area of the person's life that I found inspiring, and that I am praying you do, too, as you reflect on their character and history. The historical aspects are well researched, the commentary and themes are more subjective in nature. My goal in this book is to make your experience as authentic to my family's experience each February.

When we gathered, my family would talk through a person's history, but we couldn't read an entire autobiography or biography in one night, so here, I have provided a brief profile for you, similar to what we would have done. We would hear the voice of the person whenever and however possible. We would read a story or speech, and I've attempted to include a sample of the person's work for you. We visited the Frederick Douglass National Historic Site and the National Museum of African American History and Culture in Washington, DC, and went to the National Museum of African American Music in Nashville, Tennessee, and more. We have been intentional, and *Celebrating Around the Table* will take you into those spaces right where you are.

All of these stories are filled with heartache and hope, brokenness and redemption. I can't wait for you to explore them with me and share them with your family or community. Celebrate Black history in February. Learn and give thanks. But let's

not stop there. Ultimately, it's not a celebration of a single people, but a recognition of the diversity among God's image-bearing creatures—the diversity among every tribe, tongue, and nation for whom Jesus died.

A Special Note

Celebrating Around the Table is suitable for older teens and adults. Although it includes a kids' corner for families, it is not written for young readers. Also, my family continues to enjoy this tradition of celebrating Black History Month, and although I wrote *Celebrating Around the Table* with families in mind, it truly is for *anyone*. I hope you'll invite your friends around the table to discuss the contents of the book. You could use it in your community and neighborhood to open your door and start conversations. Also, please use this book at any time! You don't have to wait until a designated month.

The Recipes

The recipes are meant to give you a taste of common Southern African American cuisine. But remember, I am not a chef, and none of the meals will be gourmet. These recipes are for the everyday cook. And although the recipes have modern ingredients, I intentionally didn't add complicated ingredients or require special equipment. So you won't need an air fryer, smoker, emulsifier, or instant pot. What you will need are basic kitchen tools, such as a blender, measuring cups, pots and pans, and an oven. Sorry, no microwave dishes. I said easy, but not that easy! When you get to desserts, you'll notice that there are fewer recipes. The reason is simply because most desserts last longer than one day.

Who doesn't love fried chicken, right? It's a staple in the American South (where I'm from) and in other cultures all over the world. And yet I found myself tempted not to add it. Black cuisine is varied and diverse. There's a temptation to assume that Black culture is monolithic. We are quite diverse. But fried chicken *is* a part of my culture and upbringing. *Celebrating Around the Table* would not be authentic to who I am without it. I point this out to say that these dishes don't fully represent the vast and wonderful variety available to you by Black cooks. The recipes included here consist of my attempt to capture what may have been eaten by some of the people we learn about, and what was definitely eaten during my upbringing.

The People Featured

Most slaves, once free, changed their names. For example, Elizabeth Freeman was born into slavery and was called Mum Bett while enslaved. To honor these men and women and to keep things as simple as possible for discussion, I am using the name that they chose once free. I will tell you what their slave name was, but then I use the name of their choosing, even if they weren't known by that name during the period I am writing about.

One more thing: You'll notice some familiar names not included in this book. The reason is simple: Many of those left out are already familiar to most readers, and it would take a lifetime to cover every person. My hope is that this is just the beginning of your own exploration into the life and history of African Americans in this country and around the world. So, although you won't find Dr. Martin Luther King Jr. profiled, you will learn about his influence on people like gospel singer Mahalia Jackson. I'm confident you will be inspired and maybe even learn something new.

Get creative, gather together, and enjoy!

My hope is that this is just the beginning of your own exploration into the life and history of African Americans in this country and around the world.

Freedom

Frederick Douglass

Once you learn to read,
you will be forever free.[1]

Frederick Douglass was an activist, a publisher, a writer, and a prose poet. He was, for 20 years, enslaved in the American South. He was a tireless speaker and accomplished rhetorician. He was the most famous African American of his lifetime, well known not just in the United States but around the world. By the end of his life, he had the ears of presidents and politicians, and had held posts in the federal government. But he was also a father, a husband, and a man who forever bore the scars of his traumatic past.

Life and Impact

As I write this introduction, there are a few things I know about myself. I was born in North Carolina in 1978, and therefore I'm—you can do the math—years old. One of the most striking evidences of the sheer horror of slavery is in the opening of Douglass's autobiography, *Narrative of the Life of Frederick Douglass, an American Slave*:

> I was born in Tuckahoe, near Hillsborough, and about twelve miles from Easton, in Talbot county, Maryland. I have no accurate knowledge of my age, never having seen any authentic record containing it. By far the larger part of the slaves know as little of their ages as horses know of theirs.[2]

Christians believe that every person is made in the image of God (Genesis 1:27). This designation is not something man-made—God chose to create every person in every tribe, tongue, and nation in His image. Our value is rooted in the blessing of the Creator of the universe. To strip someone of the knowledge of their age and put them at the level of an animal is one of the many atrocious acts of slavery. The psychological impact of a young boy feeling like an animal—the ones that God gave man dominion over—can only be compounded by being born into a system that allowed another person to own you.

Douglass as a Slave

Frederick Douglass was born Frederick Augustus Washington Bailey in Maryland around 1818. His mother was Harriet Bailey, and his father is unknown, but presumed to be white and possibly his master. Douglass and his mother's other children were taken from her at a young age. He reflected on his mother's state: "My poor mother, like many other slave-women, had many children but NO FAMILY!"[3]

As we'll see in the other profiles in this book, separating families—men, women, and children—was a customary practice. As a result of these separations, as well as the lack of record-keeping of slaves, many African Americans today cannot trace their ancestry. And we who live today will never fully understand the depths of the damage done to the families separated throughout the 300-plus years of slavery in the United States.

Despite this trauma, Douglass saw how a providential move changed his life. At the age of eight, he was loaned to a relative of his owner in Baltimore, a decision that proved pivotal in his life. He would later write,

> It is possible, and even quite probable, that but for the mere circumstance of being removed from that plantation to Baltimore, I should have to-day, instead of being here seated by my own table, in the enjoyment of freedom and the happiness of home, writing this Narrative, been confined in the galling chains of slavery.[4]

Baltimore was a world apart from the country plantations Douglass had known up to that point in his life.

At the time of Douglass's arrival, the bustling port city had a population of nearly 80,000 people, including more than 14,000 free Blacks, the largest concentration of free persons of color in the United States, and a growing number of European immigrants. Thus Douglass was able to imagine a different way of life in the world. It was here in Baltimore that Douglass learned how to read, trading bread for lessons from some of the poor Irish immigrant children on his street, and it was here that Douglass vowed he would not always remain a slave.

Unfortunately, when Douglass was about 15, his time in Baltimore was cut short; he was sent back to his owner, Thomas Auld, in rural Maryland. From there he was loaned to two other white farmers—one exceedingly cruel, the other less so but still unjust, and the relative leniency only made Douglass long more to be his own master.

When Douglass was 17, he and four friends planned an escape, only to be thwarted at the last moment. But instead of selling Douglass to someone in the Deep South, as was customary with slaves who tried to fight for freedom, Thomas Auld decided to send Douglass back to his brother Hugh in Baltimore to learn a trade—another circumstance that would prove good in Douglass's life. However, his improved circumstances did not satisfy him. A couple years later, with the help of a free Black woman named Anna Murray, 20-year-old Douglass made his escape north.

Freedom for All

After arriving safely in New York disguised as a free Black sailor, Douglass wrote to Murray, who joined him in New York. The two were married shortly thereafter and moved to Massachusetts to begin their new life. They would eventually have five children together, four of whom lived to adulthood. In New England, Douglass began to hone his oratory skills as a lay preacher for a local Black congregation and became involved in abolitionist organizations. And in 1841, Douglass gave a stirring speech at the Massachusetts Anti-Slavery Society convention before a mostly white audience.

At the end of his autobiography *Narrative*, Douglass wrote of that moment that launched his mission:

I felt strongly moved to speak, and was at the same time much urged to do so by Mr. William C. Coffin, a gentleman who had heard me speak in the colored people's meeting at New Bedford. It was a severe cross, and I took it up reluctantly. The truth was, I felt myself a slave, and the idea of speaking to white people weighed me down. I spoke but a few moments, when I felt a degree of freedom, and said what I desired with considerable ease. From that time until now, I have been engaged in pleading the cause of my brethren—with what success, and with what devotion, I had I leave those acquainted with my labors to decide.[5]

At the young age of twenty-one, Douglass was tapped to join the abolitionist speaking circuit, a role that would eventually carry him through all the northern states, from Maine to Michigan, as well as overseas to Ireland and Great Britain.

Douglass soon earned international fame as an abolitionist, author, orator, and editor. He wrote *Narrative*, the first of his three memoirs and a work of impressive literary skill, in 1844, when he was about 27 years old and it was published in 1845. In 1847, he started an abolitionist newspaper called *The North Star*, whose motto was "Right is of no Sex—Truth is of no Color—God is the Father of us all, and we are all brethren."[6] The name paid homage to the North Star, used by slaves to escape north. The paper was published in Rochester, New York, where Douglass and his family had moved, and eventually became one of the most influential abolitionist papers of its time.

One remarkable aspect of Douglass's freedom was his desire to change the narrative for all Black people. He is known to be the most photographed American of the nineteenth century—a superlative that he cultivated.[7] He believed that serious photographs of him could help counter ignorant and demeaning caricatures of Black people.[8] Racism has never been exclusive to the South; in the North, Douglass was forever fighting against patronizing stereotypes as well as outright racism. In his many travels, he accumulated countless stories of mistreatment and discrimination at the hands of hotel operators, train conductors, churches, and violent mobs. In typical fashion, Douglass channeled his indignation over these events into rousing speeches and biting editorials.

Hand in hand with Douglass's activism was his solid grounding in the Bible. He saw his own story and the story of African Americans reflected in the words of the Hebrew prophets. Upon receiving his freedom, he joined the African Methodist Episcopal Zion Church. This independent Black denomination was also home to Sojourner Truth and Harriet Tubman. Douglass became a licensed preacher in 1839, and was a tireless critic of hypocrisy in many white churches, which was likely because of a deep and genuine faith that informed his actions and his moral philosophy.

The end of Douglass's life was notably hard. His home in Rochester burned down in 1872, after which he moved to Washington, DC. Following the death of his wife, Anna, he married a white woman named Helen Pitts, nearly 20 years his junior. This caused a lot of controversy from every side of the political and social spectrum. Douglass responded by saying that his first marriage had been to someone the color of his mother and his second marriage was to someone the color of his father.[9]

Douglass worked relentlessly by continuing to fill his calendar with speaking engagements, now in the post–Civil War era, to decry the horrors of racism and the disintegration of

Reconstruction rather than an end to slavery. This tireless work was due to financial necessity as well as passion—much of his large extended family was still financially dependent on him.

On February 20, 1895, Douglass, ever an advocate for women's equality, attended the National Council of Women—a meeting held in Washington, DC. Upon his return, Douglass suffered a massive heart attack. He was 77. The next day, over the opposition of Southern members, the US Senate voted to adjourn out of respect for him. Douglass was buried in Rochester, next to his first wife, Anna. Though he was dead, his words continued to reverberate onward to the next generation of African American activists, including Booker T. Washington and W.E.B. De Bois.[10]

Devotion

There has been a lot of confusion surrounding the presence of slavery in the Bible. Yes, slavery was a part of the ancient world. Slaves were abused, exploited, and victimized. But those who follow Christ are always to be set apart, including in the ways we treat other people. We are to be different than the world, and this was Paul's calling for those who lived in Ephesus. God does not condone slavery as an acceptable institution. The confusion often stems from a misreading of texts such as Ephesians 6:5-9:

> *Bondservants, obey your earthly masters with*
> *fear and trembling, with a sincere*
> *heart, as you would Christ, not by the way of*
> *eye-service, as people-pleasers, but*
> *as bondservants of Christ, doing the will of God from*
> *the heart, rendering service*
> *with a good will as to the Lord and not to man,*
> *knowing that whatever good*
> *anyone does, this he will receive back from the Lord,*
> *whether he is a bondservant*
> *or is free. Masters, do the same to them, and stop*
> *your threatening, knowing*
> *that he who is both their Master and yours is in*
> *heaven, and that there is no partiality with him.*

Not all slavery in the first century was equivalent to the slavery of more recent centuries. In ancient Greco-Roman culture, many slaves were indentured servants and not enslaved based on their race. Their slavery was temporary, and they were not owned by another person. Rather, they were often considered a part of the household. As the gospel spread through the ancient Roman world, there were slaves and masters who became believers and wondered how they were to interact with each other. So, in the context of Ephesians 6, it makes sense that the writer of the book of Romans, Paul, would address the relationship between slaves and masters.

But no matter what kind of slavery we are talking about, it is important to note that Paul's words about how masters and slaves should relate to one another were written to help those who, in the context of a pagan culture, had become believers and wondered how that might affect them. In no way did Paul command nor condone the system of slavery.

Tragically, when slavery was permitted in America, there were people who attempted to use the Bible to justify it. But to justify the torture and cruelty done to other image bearers in the name of Jesus makes no sense at all. It was an unjust system and the use and application of the Scriptures to justify chattel slavery is a heresy that has long been condemned. When we read the Bible carefully, we can conclude that God does not condone slavery as an acceptable institution.

In contrast, the Lord has much to say about loving our neighbor. As Paul writes in 1 Corinthians 16:14, we should let all that we do be done in love. God instructs His people to love. If our actions are unloving, then they can't be pleasing to God.

The faith and hope-filled cry of Douglass led him to fight his way to freedom. His *Narrative of the Life of Frederick Douglass* continues to educate us about the real life of slaves, their owners, and their faith. The Bible reminds us of the true hope we have in the gospel, even in the midst of a broken and at times treacherous world.

Today, we can thank the Lord for the end of chattel slavery in the United States. But there's still a need for us to learn, remember, and fight for peace. The ideals of America's founding documents have not yet been fully realized. There's hope, but it is found not in our nation, but in God. If we can remember and learn from our past and the treatment of men like Frederick Douglass, then and only then will we begin to understand the depths of sorrow experienced by many in our country today.

Celebrating
Around the Table

Discussion Questions

1. What part of Frederick Douglass's story surprised, challenged, or inspired you?

2. What brings you hope about Douglass's story?

3. Douglass leaned on the Bible for strength. Why do you think that is? How might you learn from him and lean on God's Word for strength today?

4. What does freedom mean to you, and how might it change the way you live?

5. **KIDS' CORNER:** When a person owns another person, that is called chattel slavery. Why is it wrong to own another human being?

Prayer

Say a word of praise to the Lord that chattel slavery came to an end in the United States. Ask the Lord to help you understand the Scriptures in their context and apply them appropriately to your life.

Elizabeth Freeman

Any time, any time while I was a slave, if one minute's freedom had been offered to me, and I had been told I must die at the end of that minute, I would have taken it.[1]

You've heard the saying, "Practice what you preach." As stories would have it, Mum Bett would hear the words of the Declaration of Independence read after the Revolutionary War and declare, in not so many words, "America must practice what it preaches." The story goes that Mum Bett heard the words "all men are created equal," and that lit a fire in her that would lead to a fight for freedom. Once she was free, she named herself Elizabeth Freeman. Let's learn the story of one woman who dared to dream of her freedom and opened the door for others to be freed as well.

Life and Impact

Freeman as a Slave

Although most of the writings about Mum Bett are consistent, many are secondhand stories that don't come from her directly. Primary sources (text or audio directly from the subject) are scarce, especially for those who were enslaved. Unlike many of the freed slaves featured in this book, Freeman didn't write or preach. She cared for the homes of others her entire life. Slavery stripped many of their dignity, and the lack of public records is one of the many ways that happened. Many African Americans struggle to trace their lineage back beyond certain generations because there are no records that their ancestors existed. Thankfully, court records and other writings have preserved the legacy of Elizabeth Freeman.

Elizabeth Freeman was born into slavery, and although her birthplace is unknown, she ended up enslaved in the new Commonwealth of Massachusetts—this was also where she began to be called Mumbet (also known as Mum Bett). Many equate slavery with the South, but as historian Ben Z. Rose wrote, "Some of the region's most prominent families made their fortunes carrying human cargo, as New England became the nexus of North American's slave trade." Rose added, "Those who opposed slavery were few in number, and their voices were absorbed in a whirlwind of indifference."[2] Freeman was born in the mid-eighteenth century some 200 years after the start of the dreadful slave trade that devastated African people and separated families. Such is the case of Elizabeth Freeman.

At some point during her childhood, Freeman was brought as a slave into the home of John Ashley along with her sister. Their origin stories are unknown, but it is clear that they were servants to the wealthy resident and judge of Sheffield, Massachusetts, and his wife, Hannah. Freeman became an invaluable servant to Hannah and made a good name for herself throughout the town. She had been described as strong, courageous, humble, and compassionate. These characteristics, along with her tenacity and willingness to persevere, likely helped her fight for her freedom, which she won in 1781.

Freedom for All

Slavery was still in effect in Massachusetts in 1780, but the state had just adopted a new constitution that allowed for judges to review the use of slave ownership. Elizabeth's case, *Brom and Bett v. Ashley*, was heard in 1781 and was a challenge to the existence of slavery in Massachusetts. What's fascinating is that the suit may have originated from Freeman using Ashley's views against him! He was a staunch supporter of the Massachusetts Constitution and had meetings in his home, where Freeman would overhear him vocally supporting that all men were born free and equal.

It is said that Freeman overheard Ashley discussing a document he helped write called the Sheffield Declaration, which addressed promises of liberty and essentially the dignity of men. It is also said that Hannah Ashley physically abused her after attempting to burn Freeman's sister. It was then that Freeman reached out to a lawyer and began the journey toward freedom.[3]

Freeman's lawyer, Theodore Sedgwick, argued that slavery was against the Massachusetts Constitution, and won! After securing her freedom, she changed her legal name to Elizabeth Freeman and began working in the household of her attorney, where she remained until her death in 1829.

Freeman was buried in the Sedgwick family plot. The words engraved on her tombstone encapsulate her character:

She was born a slave and remained a slave for nearly thirty years. She could neither read nor write yet in her own sphere she had no superior or equal. She neither wasted time nor property. She never violated a trust nor failed to perform a duty. In every situation of domestic trial, she was the most efficient helper, and the tenderest friend. Good mother, farewell.[4]

Freeman is known as the first African American woman to win her freedom in a court in the United States. Her fight was not just for herself, but for the freedom and liberty of all people. The dignity that others attempted to strip away from her never diminished. She hoped for one minute of freedom and received it until her passing at approximately 85 years of age.

Devotion

*God created man in his own image, in the image of God he
created him; male and female he created them (Genesis 1:27).*

The Lord did something remarkable—astonishing, in fact—when,
after creating plants, oceans, light and darkness, animals, and
everything we love to explore in the world, He created people.
He created us with the ability to reflect Him. You and I are made
in the image of God. We are set apart from all of creation as the
only creatures that bear His image. We were all made to reflect
the Lord, and we can do this most clearly by displaying God's
communicable attributes (the attributes that we can emulate).

God's communicable attributes are those moral characteristics that you and I should strive to exhibit—like His love, gentleness, patience, kindness, and goodness. But even when we aren't
trying to reflect these attributes, we have the potential to do so
because we were created by God. He has given every human His
image, which means that even if a person doesn't acknowledge
that they were created by God, he or she still reflects Him!

Think about the graciousness of this act of God and the impli-
cations of it. Everyone is created with intrinsic value and worth.
Everyone. This is equally true of all of us. We are born valuable.
We are born with forethought by our Creator God. "You formed
my inward parts; you knitted me together in my mother's
womb" refers to us all (Psalm 139:13). This should be cause for

great rejoicing. The problem with chattel slavery and the experience of Elizabeth Freeman and every person made in the image of God who endured slavery is there were many who refused to acknowledge this glorious truth.

We are created equally in God's image. He doesn't discriminate in His design. In other words, He doesn't create one human being greater than another. We ought to treat others in a manner worthy of this reality. We should reflect God's character to those around us. We should display kindness, gentleness, love, and patience toward all. Every person, from every tribe, tongue, and nation, is valuable to God, and therefore should be valuable to you and me.

Discussion Questions

1. What part of Elizabeth Freeman's story surprised, challenged, or inspired you?

2. Have you ever considered that descendants of slaves have little to no record of their ancestors? Can you see how the lack of records can be dehumanizing and why African Americans may still be affected by this today?

3. If you are an African American, how have you grappled with the matter of ancestors?

4. How might understanding the fact we are all created in the image of God help us to interact with and think about those not like us?

5. How does knowing we're made in the image of God help us to realize the importance of the fruit of the Spirit in Galatians 5:22-23?

6. **KIDS' CORNER:** Did you know that you are made in the image of God? That means you are made to reflect God. Because He is good, you can be good too. Who else is made in the image of God?

Prayer

Thank the Lord for His kindness and generosity in making you in His image. Ask the Lord to help you see others as being made in His image too.

Harriet Tubman

I said to the Lord, "I'm going to hold steady on to you, and I know you will see me through."[1]

Harriet Tubman is likely one of the more recognizable names of the abolitionist movement along with Frederick Douglass and Sojourner Truth. We know of her heroic feats. We've heard the stories of the Underground Railroad, where she helped rescue approximately 70 people.[2] But did you know that she was a devout Christian, had a brain injury and suffered until her death, was a spy, joined a colonel in the Union Army to free more than 700 slaves, was a nurse, and was married? Tubman lived a long life of service to others.

Life and Impact

Tubman as a Slave

Harriet Tubman was born between 1819 and 1823 in Dorchester County, Maryland. She was born into slavery and named Araminta ("Minty") Ross. Tubman was one of nine children all born to Harriet "Rit" (mother) and Ben Ross (father). Tubman's parents were bought and separated; therefore, Tubman did not get to know her father. Eventually, Tubman also witnessed two of her siblings being sold off too. The little time she did have with her mother was fruitful. Tubman's parents had strong faith and taught their children about the Lord.

Tubman's biographer, Sarah Bradford, wrote of Tubman's faith:

> Hers was not the religion of a morning and evening prayer at stated times, but when she felt a need, she simply told God of it, and trusted him to set the matter right.[3]

Tubman recalled a time when she prayed for her master. She said,

> As I lay so sick on my bed, from Christmas till march, I was always praying for poor ole master..."Oh, Lord, convert ole master"; "Oh dear Lord, change dat man's heart, and make him a Christian." But she also prayed that if her master wasn't going to do good, that he would die.[4]

We don't know when Harriet came to know the Lord, but we do know that she did, and she proclaimed Him to those around her. She considered the Lord her friend and spoke to Him as such. She would talk to Him and had confidence not only that He heard her, but that He cared for her too. It was her faith that helped her through the trials and suffering she would soon endure.

At the tender age of 13 years old, Tubman was nearly killed when she was struck in the head by a large object. The details of the story vary, but we know that an angry slave owner threw a heavy metal object in a fit of rage, and it hit Tubman. The injury caused irreparable damage for that time in history and pressure on the brain. Tubman suffered headaches, narcolepsy, and seizures for the remainder of her life. Tubman said the injury also gave her dreams and visions, which she attributed to God.

During one of Tubman's potential seizures or fits, as her biographer, Sarah Bradford, called them, the men Tubman worked for whipped her, leaving lashes on her young, frail body. This had been done in a poor attempt to control her. But as Bradford noted, "If they had only known it, the touch of a gentle hand upon her shoulder, and her name spoken in tones of kindness, would have accomplished what cruelty failed to do."[5]

Tubman endured terrible treatment as a young woman. She worked with little to no instruction and would be punished when she did something that her masters considered to be wrong. She was whipped for falling asleep while rocking a baby at night because the baby woke the mother. Even at the age of 60 she still wore the scars inflicted by her oppressors. Tubman recalled hearing the cries of other slaves being tortured and asked herself, "Why should such things be? Is there no deliverance for my people?"[6]

At some point, Tubman was sold to a cruel man who made her lift heavy barrels of flour and other goods. As happens in so many of these stories, what man planned for evil, the Lord planned for good. As she was lifting and carrying those heavy loads, she was building strength for the journey and task ahead of her.

Freedom for All

When Tubman was in her twenties, she and two of her brothers decided to try to escape. She heard that her owner planned to sell her to a Southern state, and she knew she must flee. She took off, but her brothers turned back. Tubman carried on, making her way to the north using the stars as her guide. By the time of her escape in 1849, Minty Ross was married to John Tubman,[7] a free African American man, and was already going by Harriet Tubman. This would mean that Tubman left behind her husband and entire family to escape the jaws of slavery. Tubman used the Underground Railroad to escape, and would one day become a conductor to help others escape too.

The Underground Railroad was a not an actual railroad, and it wasn't under the ground. It operated as a network of people, African American and white, who provided homes, wagons, churches, schoolhouses, and more to help guide escaped slaves to safety. "Conductors" were guides like those you would see on a hiking trail, but with greater significance. People would hear about the meeting places and go, which is what Tubman did to escape.

The Fugitive Slave Acts made escaping and staying free difficult for ex-slaves. These federal laws allowed for the capture and return of runaway enslaved people within the territory of the United States. This meant that although many slaves escaped to the North, the North wasn't always safe. Some escapees went as far as Canada, where they would be truly free. Bounties would be placed on the heads of escaped slaves, which made it lucrative for people to capture and return a slave. One such bounty was now on Tubman's head. She received assistance from others, and she would soon provide help to her people as well. Assisting runaway slaves was a risk and punishable by law, which is why most of the journeys took place in the dead of night.

Tubman made her way to Philadelphia, where the population of Black people was upwards of 20,000. Philadelphia was home to the Pennsylvania Society for the Promotion of the Abolition of Slavery, a historical and committed group of abolitionists. Philadelphia seemed to be a good place for an escaped slave.[8] This isn't to say living there was easy. The city was crowded, racism was prevalent, bounties were still a problem, and work was hard to come by for many.

As a free woman, Tubman found work and began to provide for herself. But loneliness and a deep desire to see her family freed stirred her to action. Tubman began to learn more about the Underground Railroad system and decided she needed to return to Maryland to help her family escape.

Tubman was a strong and courageous woman. She saved the money she earned so she could travel back to Maryland. Bradford expounded:

> All her wages were laid away with this sole purpose, and as soon as a sufficient amount was secured, she disappeared from her Northern home, and as suddenly and mysteriously she appeared some dark night at the door of one of the cabins on the plantation, where a trembling band of fugitives, forewarned as to time and place were anxiously awaiting their deliverer.[9]

Tubman guided men, women, and children through rugged terrain, up mountains, across dangerous streams of water, and often in the pitch black of night. The journey was toilsome but worth it. Harriet made this trip back and forth at least 13 times. Her first trip was in 1850, and she continued conducting in the Underground Railroad for ten years. Editor and founder of the abolitionist newspaper *The Liberator*, William Lloyd Garrison, famously called Tubman "Moses," after the biblical man who led the Israelites out of bondage in Egypt and into the Promised Land.[10]

Tubman's service went beyond the Underground Railroad. In June 1863, she became the first woman to head up a successful military raid, carried out by Union colonel James Montgomery. Tubman and 150 African American Union soldiers freed more than 700 slaves in what became known as the Combahee Ferry Raid. Before the raid, Tubman met John Brown, a freedom fighter and antislavery activist, and it is possible that they met through Frederick Douglass, another abolitionist and a friend of Tubman's. Nevertheless, they met and teamed up for armed revolution. Though Brown's raid ultimately failed, Tubman was forever grateful for his sacrifice and service.[11]

There is much more that could be said of Harriet Tubman and her remarkable life. She was also a Union spy and a nurse for African American soldiers, and she fought for women's rights. She remarried and adopted a baby girl. She founded a nursing home for African Americans in Auburn, New York. We could go on because she did. She served until her death from pneumonia on March 10, 1913. She was 93 years old.

You and I will surely be in situations where we'll need to decide whether our association with Jesus is worth being shunned by our co-workers, family, and community.

Devotion

By faith Moses, when he was born, was hidden for three months by his parents, because they saw that the child was beautiful, and they were not afraid of the king's edict. By faith Moses, when he was grown up, refused to be called the son of Pharaoh's daughter, choosing rather to be mistreated with the people of God than to enjoy the fleeting pleasures of sin. He considered the reproach of Christ greater wealth than the treasures of Egypt, for he was looking to the reward. By faith he left Egypt, not being afraid of the anger of the king, for he endured as seeing him who is invisible. By faith he kept the Passover and sprinkled the blood, so that the Destroyer of the firstborn might not touch them (Hebrews 11:23-28).

There are many times when I sit down to listen to a friend as she shares her struggles that I think to myself, *Even though I'm not in that circumstance, I can relate to her general experience.* I don't usually state that because to do so isn't always helpful. And, of course, I'm not able to relate in every way—only Jesus can. However, temptations and many circumstances are often common to most people. But when I read about the life of Moses, there's little at face value that I can imagine any of us relating to. However, it isn't hard to imagine Harriet Tubman relating to him, and after reading her story, I can see why she was named "the Moses of her people."

There isn't space here to cover all the events in the life of Moses, but we find a short overview in Hebrews 11:23-28: At the time of Moses's birth, the ruler of Egypt felt threatened by Israel and issued an order for the midwives to kill any son born to a Hebrew woman. The midwives didn't comply because they feared the Lord. So Pharaoh ordered his people to cast the male babies into the Nile (Exodus 1:15-17, 22). Moses was born during this time, and his mom, a Jewish woman, hid him from Pharaoh so he would not be killed.

There came a time when Moses could no longer be hidden, so his mother, accompanied by his sister, put him in a basket to hide him on the riverbank of the Nile. This is where the birth and early childhood of Moses gets wild. Pharaoh's daughter went to the bank of the river to bathe and noticed the basket. Moses's sister approached the woman, which would have been risky, given that Moses's sister was one of the outcasts. She asked if she could assist the woman in finding someone to nurse the child. Pharaoh's daughter agreed, and so the sister went to get their mother. In the end, Moses's mom ended up getting paid to nurse her son (Exodus 2:3-9).

As the adopted son of Pharaoh's daughter, Moses lived a lavish life, free from the threat of slavery as was common for the Hebrews, and with enormous privileges. However, as Moses grew, so did his burden for his people (the Hebrews). At one point, Moses even killed an Egyptian, intervening to protect a Hebrew as the Egyptian beat the man. Pharaoh found out about this and sought to kill Moses, who fled (Exodus 2:11-15).

These are only a few areas of the beginning of Moses's life that are highlighted by the writer of Hebrews...and what a life! But in Hebrews 11, we see an incredible aspect of Moses's faith, one that we all might face when we proclaim Jesus. Moses denied his adopted status and material positions—those were fleeting pleasures—and instead *chose* to be mistreated (Hebrews 11:25). His faith was great because of what he did in adversity for the cause of the Lord (verse 26).

We may not have the same experiences as Moses, but we can share in his faith in the face of rejection and by shining a light on our allegiance to Jesus. That's what Tubman did. Moses's actions were countercultural and endangered him. Her actions could have cost Tubman her life. Her motivation was God. Moses's was too. You and I will surely be in situations where we'll need to decide whether our association with Jesus is worth being shunned by our coworkers, family, and community.[12] As singer and songwriter Andrew Peterson eloquently asks, "Is He Worthy?"[13] He is!

Discussion Questions

1. What part of Harriet Tubman's story surprised, challenged, or inspired you?

2. We can't overlook the bravery of all the women present at the beginning of Moses's life. How do you see bravery in the life of Harriet Tubman?

3. How might God be calling you to live bravely on behalf of others?

4. Moses showed compassion on his people and defended the oppressed. Although we should never take justice into our own hands and become vigilantes, there are ways we can exercise justice on the earth. What are some practical ways you can pursue justice for others?

5. What might God be calling you to sacrifice for the sake of Christ?

6. **KIDS' CORNER:** Moses was rejected. Ms. Tubman was rejected. Did you know that Jesus was rejected too? When someone is rejected, it means they are not included, or left behind, or treated poorly. How were Moses, Harriet Tubman, and Jesus rejected? How can you make sure not to reject others?

Prayer

Pray that the Lord will give you the courage and faith to stand in the face of rejection. Ask God to help you be or become a welcoming place.

Recipes

MEAL 1

Beef Stew 56

Corn Bread 59

Homemade Butter 60

MEAL 2

One-Dish Chicken
and Stuffing 61

Boiled Green Beans 62

MEAL 3

Meat Loaf 63

Roasted Root
Vegetables 64

Salad (no recipe)

DESSERT:

Red Velvet Cake with
Cream Cheese Icing 65

Beef Stew

Beef stew reminds me of a Sunday supper. It's an easy one-pot dish, simple enough for just about anyone to make—past or present.

Ingredients

2 T. flour

Salt and pepper, to taste

2 to 3 lbs. beef stewing meat cut into 1 inch pieces

2 T. oil

1 white or yellow onion, chopped

3 cloves garlic, minced

1 lb. potatoes, peeled and cubed (yellow or gold is my preference, but any potato is fine)

3 whole carrots, peeled and chopped or sliced, or 1 (16 oz.) bag baby-cut carrots

1½ tsp. Italian seasoning

1½ tsp. garlic powder

6 cups broth (beef or chicken)

Directions

Place the flour in a bowl or resealable freezer bag. Add the salt and pepper (approximately 1 teaspoon of each). Add the beef to the bowl or bag and toss it gently to coat.

In the meantime, warm the oil on low heat in a large stockpot or Dutch oven. Once the oil is warm, add the flour-coated beef and stir it gently until all sides are brown. Add the onion and garlic to the pot and stir until fragrant (about 2 minutes), then incorporate the potatoes and carrots. Mix in the Italian seasoning and garlic powder. Finish off by pouring the broth on top of the beef and vegetables. Stir. Add a pinch of salt and pepper, to taste.

Cover and cook on low until the beef is tender (approximately 2 hours). Alternately, throw it in the slow cooker on low for 4 to 6 hours.

MEAL 1

Corn Bread

A box of Jiffy corn bread mix goes a long way in my home. So don't be afraid to pull it out and use it. But for our purposes, let's cook it up from scratch. This is a delicious, savory corn bread. Today's cooks don't often have grease just sitting around, but my mom always did. It was typically bacon fat. This recipe calls for bacon grease or Crisco. My recipe is meant to reflect the times we are studying. But if you like your corn bread sweet, you can add a tablespoon of sugar.

Ingredients

2 eggs

2 cups buttermilk

2 cups yellow cornmeal

1 tsp. baking powder

1 tsp. baking soda

¼ cup Crisco shortening
  (or bacon grease)

Directions

Preheat the oven to 400°.

Mix the eggs and buttermilk in a bowl. Set aside.

In a separate large bowl, mix the cornmeal, baking powder, and baking soda. Add the wet ingredients and whisk until incorporated.

Add your grease of choice to a cast-iron skillet* and melt it in the oven. Once melted, remove the pan from the oven and add your corn bread mixture to the hot pan.

Return the pan to the oven and bake the corn bread for 15 to 20 minutes. Insert a toothpick or fork into the center of the corn bread to check for doneness, and pull the corn bread from the oven when the utensil comes out clean. Enjoy!

*If you do not own a cast-iron skillet, use a round cake pan. Melt the grease in the microwave and add it to the pan, then finish the recipe as directed.

Homemade Butter

You can't have corn bread without butter! Homemade butter is fairly easy to make. Enjoy!

Ingredients

1 quart (32 oz.) heavy whipping cream

1 tsp. salt (optional)

Directions

Pour the heavy cream into the bowl of an electric stand mixer. Turn the mixer on at medium speed and leave it on for several minutes.* The heavy cream will become whipped cream—just keep it going. After the whipped cream forms, you will begin to see solid chunks form. When you see liquid separate from the solids, you've got butter! Using a colander or similar tool, pour the liquid (buttermilk) off your butter. Rinse the butter with cold water. Add the butter to a bowl, then fold in the salt.

*If you are mixing by hand, mix continually until you see the mixture form into solids. Then strain and finish the process.

One-Dish Chicken and Stuffing

When I think about this dish, I think about one person: my mom! This one-pot dish was a staple in our home growing up. In fact, as I was considering the recipes I thought most reflected my upbringing and ones potentially eaten during the lifetimes of the people featured in the book, I called up my momma and she rattled off the recipe by memory. Maybe this is how food lives on—passed down from one home chef to another.

Ingredients

Precooked rotisserie chicken*

1 (12 oz.) can cream of celery

1 (12 oz.) can cream of mushroom

1 (12 oz.) can cream of onion

4 T. butter

1 stalk celery, sliced (about ½ cup)

1 cup chopped onion

2 cloves garlic, minced

1 tsp. ground sage

1 tsp. dried rosemary

2 cups chicken broth

1 (12 oz.) pkg. corn bread stuffing mix

Pinch of salt

Directions

Preheat the oven to 375°.

Remove all the chicken meat from the bones and cut it into bite-size pieces.

In a large bowl, stir together the chopped chicken, cream of celery, cream of mushroom, and cream of onion. Set aside.

In a medium pot, melt the butter over medium heat. Once the butter has melted, add the celery and onion. Cook until tender. Add the garlic and cook for 1 minute. Add the ground sage, rosemary, and chicken broth. Stir and bring to a boil. Once boiled, remove the pot from the heat and stir in the stuffing mix.

Add the stuffing and vegetables to the large bowl with the chicken mixture. Add the salt and stir well.

Spray a 9 × 13-inch pan lightly with nonstick cooking spray. Add the chicken and stuffing mix to the pan, spreading the mixture evenly. Cook for 45 minutes.

Serve.

*You can also use chicken breasts or thighs. Cook them according to standard recipes and add the meat to the dish.

Boiled Green Beans

I grew up eating soft but not mushy vegetables, so I prefer my green beans very soft. If you prefer softer green beans, use this recipe. If you prefer a firmer green bean, try the Sautéed Green Beans on page 192. For additional variations, add cooked and chopped bacon, pieces of ham, or cayenne pepper.

Ingredients

1 lb. green beans, trimmed and cut

2 cups chicken broth

1 T. olive oil

½ onion, sliced

1 garlic clove, minced

1 tsp. garlic salt

Directions

Add the green beans and broth to a pot. Boil for no more than 10 minutes or until they reach your desired texture. Drain the green beans and set them aside in a bowl. Add the olive oil, onion, and garlic to the same pot and sauté until the onion slices are slightly softening. Add the green beans and salt. Continue cooking the green beans for 3 to 4 minutes or until the onions are cooked through but not brown.

Serve and enjoy!

Meat Loaf

I don't remember a month that went by when I didn't have meat loaf growing up. Meat loaf is similar to a one-pot dish, just in a loaf pan. It would be simple enough for most people to make with few ingredients, making it also affordable. For mine, I spice it up a bit with Italian sausage!

Ingredients

1½ lbs. lean ground beef

1 lb. mild Italian sausage

1½ medium onions, chopped

4 cloves garlic, minced

1 tsp. Italian seasoning

1 tsp. seasoning salt

¾ cup sriracha ketchup
  (recipe follows)

Directions

Preheat the oven to 375°.

Line a loaf pan* with parchment paper (if using a nonstick loaf pan, no need to line).

Combine all the ingredients except the sriracha ketchup in a large mixing bowl. Use your hands to mix until the ingredients are incorporated well.

Add the meat mixture to the loaf pan. Cook for 45 minutes. Pull the loaf from the oven. Using a spatula or basting brush, add the sriracha ketchup to the top of the loaf. Although the recipe calls for ¾ cup, use as little or as much as you prefer. Place the loaf back in the oven for 20 minutes.

*This recipe can easily be divided into two loaf pans. I use two and freeze the second loaf.

Sriracha Ketchup

½ cup ketchup

¼ cup sriracha sauce

Blend the ketchup and sriracha in a small bowl. Dab to taste. If the blend is too spicy, add more ketchup. If the sriracha is too faint, add a tablespoon at a time until it has the desired taste. You may also purchase prepared sriracha ketchup at your local grocery store. Note that I do not add sugar, vinegar, and other ingredients that you might find in a meat loaf sauce because of the sugar and vinegar already present in ketchup.

Roasted Root Vegetables

A few years ago, I had the privilege of visiting Rwanda. During my time, we visited a village of women who took a pot on an outdoor stove and threw in several root vegetables. We feasted on potatoes and cava along with fresh avocado right off the trees. This is an easy and nutritious dish that utilizes what you often have on hand.

Ingredients

6 Yukon Gold potatoes, peeled and cut into pieces

5 turnips, peeled and cut into pieces

2 sweet potatoes, peeled and cut into pieces

2 carrots, skinned and cut into pieces

1 red onion, sliced

¼ cup olive oil

½ tsp. garlic powder

Salt and pepper, to taste

Directions

Preheat the oven to 400°.

Spray a 9 × 13-inch pan with nonstick cooking spray.

Add the vegetables to a freezer bag. Add the oil to the bag and shake to coat the veggies. Alternately, you can use a bowl with a lid and shake, or simply add the veggies directly to the pan and stir to coat them with the oil.

Spread the vegetables in the prepared pan and sprinkle them with the garlic powder, salt, and pepper. Bake in the oven for 40 minutes or until the veggies are tender, stirring halfway through to recoat them with oil.

Red Velvet Cake with Cream Cheese Icing

Red Velvet Cake is really just chocolate cake with red dye. But for some reason it's transformed into something so moist and delicious that you forget that it really isn't anything more than a chocolate cake. It's my mom's favorite dessert, so like many of the dishes in this book, I had it often growing up.

Ingredients

For the cake

2⅔ cups cake flour

⅓ cup cocoa

1 tsp. baking soda

¼ tsp. salt

1 stick butter, softened

1¾ cup sugar

2 eggs

½ cup canola oil

6 tsp. (1 oz.) red food coloring

1 tsp. white vinegar

1 tsp. vanilla extract

1 tsp. rum extract

For the icing

1 (8 oz.) pkg. cream cheese, softened

1 stick (½ cup) butter, softened

2 tsp. vanilla*

3 cups powdered sugar, sifted

Pinch of salt

*Vanilla extract is a standard ingredient in most desserts, especially frosting. I love to mix it up with other flavors, such as orange, almond, or peppermint.

Directions

Preheat the oven to 350°.

In a large bowl add the cake flour, cocoa, baking soda, and salt. Whisk until blended. Set aside.

Using an electric stand mixer with a bowl or a hand mixer, add the butter and sugar to a mixing bowl and blend well, about 3 to 4 minutes. Add the eggs and blend until fully incorporated. Add the oil, food coloring, vinegar, and extracts. Blend well.

Mix the dry ingredients and wet ingredients together, alternating until all ingredients are blended. Scrape the sides of the bowl as needed.

Pour the cake batter into a Bundt pan, turning the pan to ensure the batter is spread evenly.

Bake for 60 minutes or until a toothpick inserted in the center comes out clean.

As the cake cools, prepare the frosting.

Once the cake has fully cooled, place cake on a plate and spread frosting until fully covered.

Cream Cheese Icing

Add cream cheese, butter, and vanilla to an electric mixer and mix on medium until cream cheese is incorporated and mixture is smooth. Adjust mixer to low and slowly add powdered sugar 1 cup at a time. Once frosting is smooth, add to cooled cake.

Mission

Betsey Stockton

*Are these, thought I, the beings with whom
I must spend the remainder of my life! They
are men and have souls—was the reply which
conscience made.*[1]

When a revival broke out at the College of New Jersey (now known as Princeton University), the Lord set in motion a plan only He knew about: Betsey Stockton would become a pioneer in the modern missionary movement. Stockton was a domestic slave for the wife of the president of the College of New Jersey, Reverend Ashbel Green. She was granted permission to take classes at the college. During one semester, she professed faith in Jesus and was baptized at Princeton's First Presbyterian Church. From domestic slave to college educator, and from teacher to missionary, Stockton lived an extraordinary life of service and care to others.

Life and Impact

Betsey Stockton was born around 1798. Like many of the emancipated, freed, or ex-slaves profiled in these pages, records or writings about her are hard to come by. Stockton did leave behind a journal, which we will soon read a few samplings from. She was also the slave of a powerful man in Princeton, New Jersey, which provides context for the start of her miraculous life.

At a young age, Stockton entered the home of Reverend Ashbel Green, possibly as property inherited by his wife. Remarkably, she was able to study and read in his library. It appears she may have also taken evening classes at the College of New Jersey. In 1815, a revival broke out and touched every part of that school, including Stockton. Although this was the beginning of Stockton's faith journey, it wouldn't be until 1816 that she would convert to Christianity through the ministry of seminary student Eliphat Wheeler Gilbert.[2]

Prior to her conversion to Christianity, likely during her teen years, Stockton was emancipated but stayed in the Green household as a paid domestic servant. She taught Black children in the Princeton community and attended a class that was taught by a seminary student. Stockton knew early on in her faith that she wanted to be a missionary—to Africa. But the Lord had other plans. While living with the Greens, Stockton began a friendship with Charles Samuel Stewart, who was a student of Green's. Stewart would go on to graduate from Princeton Theological Seminary, but the friendship he had forged with Stockton was deep and enduring. He encouraged Stockton to join him on a missionary journey to the Pacific in association with the American Board of Commissioners for Foreign Missions (ABCFM).

In *The Journal of Presbyterian History*, writer John Andrew reflected on the motive of the ABCFM:

> Seeking to promote Christian principles, directors of the American Board of Commissioners for Foreign Missions sent a black to labor with whites among the Sandwich Island natives. They did so because she fulfilled the qualifications of a Christian Missionary not because she was black. But her appointment reflected visions of a Christian Society far beyond those held by most Americans. Instead of being too conservative for their times, they were, indeed, almost too radical.[3]

There were many reasons for concern. Slavery was still raging throughout the States. And, of course, this was a missionary journey, and although many of their plans were practical in nature (education, assisting with agricultural needs, etc.), the ultimate goal was to share the Christian teachings about Jesus. Perhaps the faith of Stockton and the actions of the ABCFM were too radical for society in general, but they were not too radical for the mission. On November 19, 1822, Stockton was among 14 men and women to take off for the Sandwich Islands.

The Mission

We don't have much information about Stockton's life, but she did keep a journal of the missionaries' often treacherous journey across the Pacific. Even through the tempestuous seas, she endured in faith and praised the Lord.

Three days into her journey, on November 23, 1822, she wrote:

> Saturday morning at daybreak shipped a sea. The water rushed into the cabin. I saw it with very little fear; and

felt inclined to say, The Lord reigneth, let us all rejoice. I was so weak that I was almost unable to help myself. At 10 o'clock I went on deck: the scene that presented itself was, to me, the most sublime I ever witnessed. How, thought I, can "those who go down to the sea in ships" deny the existence of God. The day was spent in self-examination. This, if ever, is the time to try my motives in leaving my native land. I found myself at times unwilling to perish so near my friends; but soon became composed, and resigned to whatever should be the will of my Heavenly Father. I believed that my motives were pure: and a calm and heavenly peace soon took possession of my breast. Oh that it were always with me as it is this day![4]

Throughout her journal, Stockton wrote fondly of Sabbath days of rest, Bible reading, and gathering for church with the other passengers. As she noted above of her "self-examination," there were several times when she lamented the state of her sin and thanked the Lord for His grace. She had a sense of her need for God's mercy even as she was on a journey to serve Him. From all accounts, Stockton was a humble servant of the Lord.

On December 30, she wrote:

> Sabbath. Had prayer meeting in the morning, and preaching in the afternoon at 4 o'clock. Mr. Stewart preached from 1 Cor. i. 23. I enjoyed the Sabbath very much, and thought I felt something of the love of God in my heart. But still I felt as if I was declining in the spiritual life. I attended a little to the study of the Bible, and find it pleasant. Yet I find a void within my breast that is painful. The scenes which constantly present themselves to my view are new and interesting; and I find

they have a tendency to draw my mind from Him who is, or ought to be, my only joy. With the poor publican I will say, "God be merciful to me a sinner." At six in the evening, we caught two sharks, and saw a number of dolphins. The flesh of the shark is very good when young.[5]

When the missionary team arrived, they were shocked and possibly frightened at the sight of the natives. The men were naked, which surprised the team. But Stockton had compassion and saw their humanity:

> Are these, thought I, the beings with whom I must spend the remainder of my life! They are men and have souls— was the reply which conscience made.[6]

Stockton got to work serving in Maui in a town called Lahaina, where she taught children English. She eventually helped open the first school for the poor in the community. Most people who attended school were upper class. Stockton, an ex-slave, was providing an opportunity to the less fortunate just as people had helped make a way for her. As the missionaries educated the people, the door was opened for them to teach Christian doctrine.

Stockton's life story was remarkable, but her work as a missionary wasn't always ideal. The mission that sent her, ABCFM, did not acknowledge her as a missionary, seemingly keeping her existence a secret. What seemed like a radical move by the organization, which it was, wasn't done in a completely honorable way. Also, Stockton was often lonely and became homesick. She was overworked as she cared for Stewart's family. It was good work, but it was hard. After Mrs. Harriet Stewart became sick, Stockton and the Stewart family began their long voyage home, and by 1826, they were in Cooperstown, New York.[7]

A Lifelong Servant

Although much of our focus has been on Stockton's time as a missionary in Hawaii, she continued serving others throughout the rest of her life. She eventually moved back to Princeton, New Jersey, where she predominantly served Black community members, started a school, and was committed to a local Presbyterian church. The church was established in 1840 and called the First Presbyterian Church of Colour of Princeton. The church has since changed its name to the Witherspoon Street Presbyterian Church, and it continues to honor Stockton's legacy. As Gregory Nobles observed, "Betsey Stockton helped make the church a haven for both religious instruction and general education, leading a Sunday school where children learned both scripture and literacy."[8]

Stockton remained in Princeton, New Jersey, until her death in October 1865. The more her story is told, the longer her legacy will live on here on earth. But that's not the goal of a missionary, and I imagine it wasn't Stockton's goal. Her work had eternal significance, and her legacy is one that many are enjoying together with her in heaven.

Devotion

Jesus came and said to them, "All authority in heaven and on earth has been given to me. Go therefore and make disciples of all nations, baptizing them in the name of the Father and of the Son and of the Holy Spirit, teaching them to observe all that I have commanded you. And behold, I am with you always, to the end of the age"
(Matthew 28:18-20).

Jesus's first disciples were an interesting bunch. They doubted, they asked silly questions, they were competitive, just to name a few things. They were very much like you and me! When I read the Gospels (Matthew, Mark, Luke, and John), one fact that stands out to me is that they were all ordinary. Several of them were fishermen, and one was even a tax collector (Matthew 4:19; 9:9). There appears to be little that is impressive about them. But God. God uses the ordinary to change the world!

In Matthew 28:19-20, the resurrected Lord gave the command for His disciples, and by extension, all those who follow Him, to go into the world and share the good news—and then teach those who hear it to obey all that He commands. The disciples took His words to heart, and in the book of Acts, we see them planting churches throughout the region. The disciples didn't share the gospel in a friendly, welcoming environment. Rather, they were persecuted, and some were even killed. Their desire was to go to the ends of the earth to share with anyone who would listen.

It's easy to read the stories of old and think, *Wow, they were so amazing and brave.* But the same is true for those who share the gospel today. After all, the gospel is the same—it's never changed, and it never will. The Spirit that led the disciples and Stockton to live a life of service to others is the same Spirit we have today. We don't need to have a resume, a title, or all the right words (1 Corinthians 1:17). We do need to have a willingness, a conviction, and a love for people.

Stockton had a willingness to step out in faith to share the good news, and a conviction that the commands in Matthew 28:19-20 applied to her. Not many of us will be called to traverse across the ocean or even 200 miles away from our homes. Most of us live in neighborhoods and communities with people who are similar to us. And for us to make disciples of "all nations" would be difficult due to our circumstances and surroundings. But we can make disciples around us who go on to make other disciples, who make still other disciples, who then make disciples of all nations. We can pray for God to be known among the peoples of all nations. Or maybe, just maybe, He is calling you to get up and go.

Discussion Questions

1. What part of Betsey Stockton's story surprised, challenged, or inspired you?

2. Put yourself in Stockton's shoes. Write down or discuss how you'd feel boarding a ship as the only person of your ethnic background or culture to a foreign land.

3. How do you think the way we view our fellow man affects the mission to go and make disciples of all nations (Matthew 28:19-20)?

4. Think through all the cultural differences in Stockton's story (white man shared with Stockton, Stockton learned at Princeton, Stockton boarded ship with white missionaries, Stockton met the Hawaiian natives, the natives met the white men and women, and so on). Describe how the gospel breaks down these barriers and moves people to love, acceptance, and action.

5. Throughout this book and in Stockton's story, we've seen that many people pursued ministry, writing, preaching, singing, or activism because of the support and encouragement of others. Who could you support or encourage now to take the next steps in their journey?

6. **KIDS' CORNER:** Do you know what a missionary is? What did Betsey Stockton do as a missionary?

Prayer

If you know Jesus, there's reason to praise Him. Thank the Lord for giving you saving faith so that you might know Him. If you do not know the Lord as your Savior, ask Him to give you the gift of faith and help you believe, and turn from your sin and put your trust in Jesus.

George Liele

I requested of my Lord and Master to give me a work, I did not care how mean it was, only to try and see how good I would do it...I felt such love and joy as my tongue was not able to express.[1]

George Liele has a wild and peculiar story—one that seems to require the hand of the Lord. Of course all stories are in His hands, but Liele's is one that might cause you to say to yourself, *Only the Lord could do that.*

Liele was born into slavery in 1752. His master, Henry Sharp, was a Baptist deacon and, after moving to Burke County, Georgia, began bringing Liele to church. In 1773, Liele professed faith in the Lord, and Sharp encouraged him to preach to other slaves.

Eventually Sharp decided to free Liele. Sharp went on to fight in the Revolutionary War and was killed in battle. As a free man, Liele traveled to Georgia and started a church.

Life and Impact

So how did Liele go on to become a missionary? Let's start by reading what he wrote of his conversion:

> I saw my condemnation in my own heart, and I found no way wherein I could escape the damnation of hell, only through the merits of my dying Lord and Savior Jesus Christ; which caused me to make intercession with Christ, for the salvation of my poor immortal soul; and I full well recollect, I requested of my Lord and Master to give me work, I did not care how mean it was, only to try and see how good I would do it. I felt such love and joy as my tongue was not able to express. After this I declared before the congregation of believers the work which God had done in my soul, and the same minister [who shared the gospel with me] the Rev. Matthew Moore, baptized me, and I continued in this church about four years, till the vacuation.[2]

And put to work he was. After his profession of faith, Liele endeavored to share it with as many people as he could, preaching to other slaves. He wrote:

> Desiring to prove the sense I had of my obligations to God, I endeavored to instruct my own color in the word of God the white Brethren seeing my endeavors, and that the word of the Lord seem to be blessed, gave me a call at a quarterly meeting to preach before the congregation.[3]

Liele's white pastor saw the fruit of his ministry, and the church licensed him to be a minister. Liele continued preaching to the slaves and is recognized as the first African American Baptist pastor in America. Liele's ministry grew exponentially.

But it wasn't all smooth sailing. Sharp had died while the Revolutionary War was still in full swing. Even though Sharp had given Liele papers for his freedom, some people were frustrated by Liele's freedom and threw him in jail. He quickly won his freedom, thanks to the papers Sharp had given him.

The Mission

At the end of the war, Liele fled Georgia by borrowing $700 from a colonel in the British army and paying for his way out of the States. He left Savannah as an indentured servant to the colonel, along with some evacuated British troops. In 1782, he landed in Jamaica with the troops and began a journey into ministry to the poor and enslaved. Once Liele was able to pay back the colonel, he was freed of his indentured servitude.

Liele wrote about his trip in a letter:

> I began, about September 1784 to preach in Kingston in a small private house to a good smart congregation, and I formed the church with four brethren from America besides myself and the preaching took very good effect with the poor sort, especially the slaves. The people at first persecuted us both at meetings and baptisms, but God be praised, they seldom interrupted us now. We have applied to the Honourable House of Assembly, with a petition of our distresses, being poor people, desiring to worship Almighty God according to the tenants of the Bible, and they have granted us liberty to worship him as we please in Kingston.[4]

The Lord used Liele's perseverance. His missionary and pastoral achievements would be worthy of celebration any day. But the fruit of his labors are staggering. In letters about his ministry, he wrote,

I have baptized four hundred in Jamaica. At Kingston I baptized in the sea, at Spanish Town in the river, and at covenant and at convenient places in the country. We have nigh THREE HUNDRED AND FIFTY MEMBERS; a few white people among them, one white brother of the first battalion of royals, from England, baptized by Rev. Thomas Davis. Several members have been dismissed to other churches, and twelve have died.[5]

Liele sent out other ministers to plant churches. He established a school for the children of slaves and free Black Jamaicans. He faithfully ministered and served in Jamaica for the remainder of his life. Although Liele's ministry was a huge success, he also suffered. He incurred incredible persecution from the white slave masters in the community. Beginning in the late 1790s, the persecution ramped up and Liele was targeted in such a way as to not only silence him but remove him from his public ministry altogether.

A Faithful Preacher and Sufferer

In 1797, Liele was falsely charged with inciting a rebellion through his preaching. He was acquitted, but then he was jailed again because he owed a debt on the church building. Liele remained there until the debt was paid. But even jail couldn't prevent him from preaching God's Word. While imprisoned, he continued to preach the good news to other prisoners and anyone else who would listen.

For the remainder of his ministry, Liele continued to endure great suffering, persecution, and pain. But he never stopped preaching. By the time of his death, there were more than 20,000 Baptists in Jamaica.[6]

Devotion

Those who received his word were baptized, and there
were added that day about three thousand souls.
And they devoted themselves to the apostles' teaching and
the fellowship, to the breaking of bread and the prayers...
And day by day, attending the temple together and breaking
bread in their homes, they received their food with glad and
generous hearts, praising God and having favor with all the
people. And the Lord added to their number day by day those
who were being saved (Acts 2:41-42, 46-47).

When I first became a Christian, I was so amazed by how devoted my friends were to one another. My church would host small group meetings and we would open our Bibles, discuss what we were learning, share what we were experiencing, and enjoy food. It was then that I began to understand what fellowship looked like through hospitality, and the importance of relationships in the church. The first-century church clearly understood this too.

The disciples had been given the Great Commission—Jesus had told them to go and make disciples of all nations (Matthew 28:18-20). At the beginning of Acts 2, Peter gave a powerful speech. When the people heard Peter's words, they were cut to the heart and asked, "What shall we do?" (verse 37). Peter told them to repent and be baptized. On that day, 3,000 people were added to the family of God.

Right after Peter spoke, the rest of Acts 2 focused on the need to obey God's Word and fellowship with one another. Hospitality was a major part of culture at that time, and the apostles would need the support of many helpers so they could do their missionary duties.

When I reflect on Liele's life, I can't help but think about the righteous saints who likely helped him along the way. He had to get to Jamaica. He needed help once he arrived, and especially when he endured persecution. Love compels the righteous to serve others (Matthew 25:35-36). But also, like Peter, Liele didn't stop preaching the good news in the face of adversity, and the Lord added to his numbers.

We don't always know the needs of those around us, but we do know that we can't walk out, on our own, the mission God has given us. Maybe the Lord is calling you to radical hospitality. Perhaps it starts slowly. It can be as simple as inviting another family over for one night to enjoy fellowship together while cooking a recipe that's in this book! Whatever you do, be willing to open your home and welcome others to your table.

Discussion Questions

1. What part of George Liele's story surprised, challenged, or inspired you?

2. God blessed Liele's ministry work. What are some ways we see the Lord working similarly today?

3. Although we have much to celebrate, we also have much to lament. Why?

4. Liele had supporters and partners in his work, but he was terribly persecuted. Can you think of Scripture verses that might have helped him during such times? (Hint: Look up the word *persecution* in the concordance in the back of your Bible, or check online Bible resources such as BibleHub or BibleGateway.)

5. Why do you think fellowship and hospitality are such important parts of the Christian faith? And how can our practical love for one another help add to the numbers of those who are saved?

6. KIDS' CORNER: Why do you think it is important to welcome people into your home or at your lunch table? What are some ways you can welcome people?

Prayer

Ask the Lord to help you see people and welcome them into your home or take them out to lunch. Ask Him to increase the number of people in your church—not for the sake of numbers, but because you long for more people to know Jesus.

Charlotte L. Forten Grimké

*Every kindly word, every gentle and generous deed we
bestow upon others—every ray of sunshine which penetrates
the darkness of another's life, through the opening which
our hands have made, must give to us a truer, nobler
pleasure than any self-indulgence can impart.*[1]

Education was dangerous to those who wanted to keep
enslaved men and women oppressed. Frederick Douglass
wrote, "'Very well,' thought I. 'Knowledge unfits a child to be
a slave.' I instinctively assented to the proposition, and from
that moment I understood the direct pathway from slavery
to freedom."[2]

Although I'm unsure of whether Douglass and Grimké crossed
paths, it is clear that her love for knowledge and teaching was
a benefit to her life and her legacy. She not only taught young
white children but would one day teach emancipated slaves,
helping them to achieve greater freedom and possibilities for
their futures.

Life and Impact

Unlike many of the profiles featured in *Celebrating Around the Table*, Charlotte Forten (whose name changed to Grimké after she married) was born free into a prominent and wealthy Black family during the antebellum and Reconstruction eras. She grew up in Philadelphia and never went to public school. Instead, she was tutored privately—one of the signs of her family's wealth. When her family moved to Salem, Massachusetts, Forten's privileged education continued, and in 1856, she attended the Salem Normal School for teaching. Today, the word *privilege* has a negative connotation. The reality is that Forten was indeed privileged, and she would one day use her incredible education and privilege to lift up others.

Forten kept a detailed journal, which makes it easier for us to assess her views and emotional state at the time. She lamented slavery and wrote of her opposition to it in her private journal and in public articles. In her journal, she wrote this concerning the escape of slave Anthony Burns from Virginia to Boston and his return to his master after massive protests in his favor:

> Our worst fears are realized; the decision was against poor Burns, and he has been sent back to a bondage worse, a thousand times worse than death. Even an attempt at rescue was utterly impossible; the prisoner was completely surrounded by soldiers with bayonets fixed, a cannon loaded, ready to be fired at the slightest sign. To-day Massachusetts has again been disgraced; again has she shewed her submission to the Slave Power; and Oh! with what deep sorrow do we think of what will doubtless be the fate of that poor man when he is again consigned to the horrors of Slavery.[3]

Forten was public about her opposition to slavery and became involved in the abolitionist movement. She wrote poems for the anti-slavery publication *The Liberator* and also for *The Evangelist*.[4] Unfortunately, her poetry and writings are hard to come by, but her journal is readily available. In 1856, Forten received a job offer at an all-white public school in Salem, and she continued attending anti-slavery meetings and celebrations.

The Mission

Forten struggled with illness, which kept her from her work and studies. But in 1862, she was commissioned to be a part of a mission to the Sea Islands around Beaufort, South Carolina. After an occupation by US military forces, wealthy white townspeople fled the Beaufort area, leaving formerly enslaved people to rebuild. The remaining people, government officials, and northern missionaries developed the Port Royal Experiment. Charlotte Forten was among the many teachers who made their way to the area. Forten ended up on Saint Helena Island and joined the staff of the Penn School for freed slaves.

Reflecting on her age and forthcoming trip, she wrote:

> Sunday, Aug. 17th. My twenty-fifth birthday. Tisn't a very pleasant thought that I have lived a quarter of a century, and am so very, very ignorant. Ten years ago, I hoped for a different fate at twenty-five. But why complain? The accomplishments, the society, the delights of travel which I have dreamed of and longed for all my life, I am now convinced can never be mine. If I can go to Port Royal, I will try to forget all these desires. I will pray that God and His goodness will make me noble enough to find my highest happiness in doing my duty.[5]

It is easy to praise humble servants like Forten and forget that they had to make real sacrifices. Forten's prayer that God would help her forget her desires and make her ready for her mission is commendable and convicting. Throughout her journal, we read of her clear dependence on God and often self-deprecating language. She doesn't appear to be entitled. She was young and ambitious yet focused on others.

After Forten's arrival at Saint Helena Island, she had the chance to visit the school and wrote of her visit:

> We went into the school, and heard the children read and spell. The teachers tell us that they had made great improvements in a very short time, and I noticed with pleasure how bright, how eager to learn many of them seem. The singing delighted me most. They sang beautifully in their rich, sweet clear tones, and with that peculiar swaying motion which I had noticed before in the older people, and which seems to make their singing all the more effective. Besides several other tunes they sang "Marching Along" with much spirit, and then one of their own hymns "Down in the Lonesome Valley," which is sweetly solemn and most beautiful. Dear children! born in slavery, but free at last! May God preserve to you all the blessings of freedom, and may you be in every possible way fitted to enjoy them. My heart goes out to you. I shall be glad to do all that I can to help you.[6]

Forten's first experiences at the school sound delightful, but she was also human. Journal entries tell a tale of joy, frustration, confusion, delight, and culture shock. Forten never experienced slavery, so immersing herself into the lives of former slaves was difficult.

Wednesday, Nov 5. Had my first regular teaching experience, and to you and only you friend beloved, will I acknowledge that I was *not* a very pleasant one. Part of my Scholars are very tiny—babies, I call them—and it is hard to keep them quiet and interested while I'm hearing the larger ones.[7]

And in another entry, she wrote about the color of the skin of those she interacted with. She was disturbed by a "dirty mulatto girl" that she wanted to clean. And was surprised by those who were "quite black."[8]

Humans are not one-dimensional. We are complicated, and even the most saintly among us have blind spots. Most of Forten's language toward the children was honorable and filled with respect and kindness. But her journal entries show a more complete picture of her experiences. Her greatest grievances seemed to be the disappointing cold weather she didn't escape even though she was in the South, and not the children she cared for. Nonetheless, she did experience some culture shock.

A Persistent Voice

After the Civil War, Forten continued to teach but moved to Boston, then Charleston, before settling in Washington, DC, in 1872. While in DC, she taught school for one year. Afterward, she clerked in the US Treasury Department. In 1878, she married Rev. Francis Grimké. The Grimkés had one child who died before reaching the age of one.

Forten Grimké was a force to be reckoned with. She went on to found the National Association of Colored Women and published poetry. She was an active part of the civil rights movement until she died on July 23, 1914.

The gospel changes everything about our relationships and how we interact with one another.

Devotion

He is no longer like a slave to you. He is more than a slave,
for he is a beloved brother, especially to me. Now he will
mean much more to you, both as a man and as a brother in
the Lord (Philemon 16 NLT).

We don't know how the slave Onesimus and Paul met. We don't
know how they became such good friends. But what we do know
from the book of Philemon is that Onesimus had a profound
effect on Paul, and Paul likely shared the good news of Jesus with
Onesimus. Paul rightly viewed Onesimus as a brother in Christ
and appealed to Philemon to do likewise. His proclamation was
not just a nice gesture; rather, it spoke of the reality of their new
standing with one another as believers. Onesimus was no longer
a slave; he was a brother.

The gospel changes everything about our relationships and
how we interact with one another. As Christians, we are adopted
children of God. We are children of God, heirs of God, and fellow
heirs with Christ (Romans 8:16-17). God created us, saves us, and
then He adopts us as His very own children.

Even before His death, Jesus affirmed the importance of
being a part of the family of God. Addressing a group of people while His mother and brothers wanted to speak to Him,
Jesus said, "'Who is my mother, and who are my brothers?' And
stretching out his hand toward his disciples, he said, 'Here are

my mother and my brothers! For whoever does the will of my Father in heaven is my brother and sister and mother'" (Matthew 12:48-50).

The truth of our relationship as brothers and sisters in Christ is such a radical concept. It's also a mystery. Christians all over the world with their various skin colors and languages and traditions and cultures are all part of the family of God. I imagine many Christian abolitionists understood this remarkable truth. In many ways, Forten had to grapple with this reality too. As an educated Christian with a different life experience than those enslaved, some of her writing shines a light on how we all must guard against the temptation to relate to others in a hierarchical nature, even when we are fighting for justice as she so heroically did. The gospel abolishes worldly hierarchies and makes us one in Him—brothers and sisters in Christ.

Discussion Questions

1. What part of Charlotte Forten's story surprised, challenged, or inspired you?

2. Many of those featured in this book found some form of teaching to be a major influence in their lives, whether it was the teaching of the gospel, reading books, or getting educational training. Why do you think education was so important for slaves and ex-slaves?

3. Forten loved to teach and loved her students but struggled with some of their cultural differences. She didn't run away, but instead, continued to serve and teach—she pressed in. Have you ever experienced a different culture and had a negative reaction at first? What did you do?

4. How does understanding the doctrine of adoption (we are adopted children of God and we are brothers and sisters in Christ) transform the way we relate to one another?

5. Thinking about the image of God and the astonishing reality that Christians are brothers and sisters in Christ, how does this change how we relate to one another?

6. KIDS' CORNER: Did you know that your friends at church are also your brothers and sisters in Christ? That's right! When you belong to God, you also belong to God's family.

Prayer

Ask the Lord to give you eyes to see others as He sees them. Pray for opportunities to care for those who are not like you.

Recipes

MEAL 4

Black Eyed Peas 100

Greens 103

Corn Bread 104

Homemade Butter 105

MEAL 5

Baked Ribs 106

Creamy Mac
   and Cheese 107

Coleslaw (no recipe)

MEAL 6

Salmon Croquettes 108

Potato Salad 109

DESSERT:

Apple Pie 110

Black-Eyed Peas

Every New Years Day for as long as I can remember, I ate black-eyed peas, greens, and corn bread. My family now has to have it every year too. As a matter of fact, I only remember one year that I missed this meal. It was a terrible year! In all seriousness, the tradition is that this meal gives you luck. I have no idea where it came from nor do I believe in superstitions, but I do love traditions. So, we carry on!

Serve with corn bread and homemade butter (see recipes on pages 104 and 105).

Ingredients

1 lb. dried black-eyed peas

1 T. oil

4 strips bacon, chopped

1 white onion, chopped

4 cloves garlic, minced

½ T. garlic powder

4 cups chicken broth

Salt and pepper, to taste

½ tsp. cayenne pepper (optional)

Directions

Soak the peas in water overnight. Rinse and set aside.

Add the oil and bacon to a large stockpot. Fry the bacon over medium heat until it is cooked but not crispy.

Add the onion and garlic to the stockpot, cooking it until the onion is translucent. Add the peas and garlic powder and stir.

Add the chicken broth and stir. Bring the contents of the stockpot to a boil, then lower the heat and simmer the peas for 1½ hours or until tender.

Spoon 2 scoops of peas into a bowl and mash. Add the mashed peas back to the pot and stir to blend thoroughly. Add salt and pepper and optional cayenne to taste.

Serve and enjoy! (Black-eyed peas can easily serve as a main dish too!)

Greens

I could eat greens for breakfast, lunch, and dinner. These savory greens are easy to make and even better to eat. Although I used turnip greens for this recipe, collard greens work just as well.

Ingredients

2 slices bacon, cut in pieces

½ cup chopped onion

4 cloves garlic, minced

1 tsp. garlic powder

Salt and pepper, to taste

1 lb. turnip or collard greens

4 cups chicken broth

Directions

Fry the bacon in a large stockpot over medium heat until cooked through. Add the onion and garlic, cooking until the onion is translucent. Add the garlic powder, salt, and pepper.

Trim and rinse the greens, breaking them into medium-size pieces (greens will shrink significantly). Add the greens to the pot and stir. Add the broth and bring the mixture to a boil. Lower the temperature to medium and cook until the greens are tender (about 45 minutes).

Corn Bread

A box of Jiffy corn bread mix goes a long way in my home. So don't be afraid to pull it out and use it. But for our purposes, let's cook it up from scratch. This is a delicious, savory corn bread. Today's cooks don't often have grease just sitting around, but my mom always did. It was typically bacon fat. This recipe calls for bacon grease or Crisco. My recipe is meant to reflect the times we are studying. But if you like your corn bread sweet, you can add a tablespoon of sugar.

Ingredients

2 eggs

2 cups buttermilk

2 cups yellow cornmeal

1 tsp. baking powder

1 tsp. baking soda

¼ cup Crisco shortening
 (or bacon grease)

Directions

Preheat the oven to 400°.

Mix the eggs and buttermilk in a bowl. Set aside.

In a separate large bowl, mix the cornmeal, baking powder, and baking soda. Add the wet ingredients and whisk until incorporated.

Add your grease of choice to a cast-iron skillet* and melt it in the oven. Once melted, remove the pan from the oven and add your corn bread mixture to the hot pan.

Return the pan to the oven and bake the corn bread for 15 to 20 minutes. Insert a toothpick or fork into the center of the corn bread to check for doneness, and pull the corn bread from the oven when the utensil comes out clean. Enjoy!

*If you do not own a cast-iron skillet, use a round cake pan. Melt the grease in the microwave and add it to the pan, then finish the recipe as directed.

Homemade Butter

You can't have corn bread without butter! Homemade butter is fairly easy to make. Enjoy!

Ingredients

1 quart (32 oz.) heavy whipping
   cream

1 tsp. salt (optional)

Directions

Pour the heavy cream into the bowl of an electric stand mixer. Turn the mixer on at medium speed and leave it on for several minutes.* The heavy cream will become whipped cream—just keep it going. After the whipped cream forms, you will begin to see solid chunks form. When you see liquid separate from the solids, you've got butter! Using a colander or similar tool, pour the liquid (buttermilk) off your butter. Rinse the butter with cold water. Add the butter to a bowl, then fold in the salt.

*If you are mixing by hand, mix continually until you see the mixture form into solids. Then strain and finish the process.

Baked Ribs

Another Southern favorite. Most people these days like to slow cook ribs in a smoker or a grill. But for our purposes, we are going to bake them. They will turn out just as juicy.

Ingredients

2 racks of baby back ribs

2 T. store-bought jerk seasoning or favorite dry rub

1 tsp. Worcestershire sauce

1 tsp. garlic powder

1 tsp. onion powder

Splash of liquid smoke

2 T. olive oil

Directions

Line a large baking sheet with aluminum foil. Place the ribs on the baking sheet. Prepare the ribs by pulling off and discarding the white membrane.

In a small bowl, mix the jerk seasoning, the Worcestershire sauce, and the remaining seasonings. Add the oil and stir well. Rub the seasoning blend all over the ribs, then cover them loosely with aluminum foil. Place the ribs in the refrigerator for an hour or overnight.

When ready to cook, preheat the oven to 300°.

Place the covered ribs into the oven for 2 hours.

Pull the ribs from the oven and cut between the bones when ready to serve.

Creamy Mac and Cheese

This is your grandma's mac and cheese, but with a few twists. Of all the dishes in this book, I likely took the most liberties with this mac and cheese. It's creamy and delicious and made with unique cheeses. I love a good creamy mac and cheese. I hope you enjoy my smoky version of this traditional dish.

Ingredients

1 lb. elbow macaroni

4 T. butter

4 T. flour

2 cups milk

1 cup heavy cream

8 oz. sharp cheddar cheese, shredded

8 oz. fontina cheese, shredded

8 oz. smoked cheddar, shredded

7 oz. Italian blend cheese, shredded

1 tsp. onion powder

Salt and pepper, to taste

Directions

Cook the macaroni noodles according to package directions, reducing the time slightly to have al dente noodles. Drain and rinse the noodles with cold water. Stir to separate the noodles, and set aside.

Meanwhile, grease a 9 × 13-inch pan, and preheat the oven to 400°.

Melt the butter in a large saucepan over medium-low heat, stirring to ensure it doesn't scorch. Once the butter has melted, add the flour and whisk until the mixture is fully incorporated. Add the milk and cream and whisk. Set the cheddar cheese to the side. Add the other cheeses in batches, mixing well after each addition. Melt the cheese, stirring continually to produce a thick sauce. Add the noodles, onion powder, salt, and pepper to the saucepan and mix well. Taste and add more salt if needed. Pour the mixture into the prepared baking pan. Sprinkle the sharp cheddar evenly over the macaroni and cheese, using more or less as desired. Bake until the cheddar is melted but not browned, approximately 25 minutes.

Serve hot. Enjoy!

Salmon Croquettes

The origin of salmon croquettes is fuzzy. All I ever knew growing up is that dried bread crumbs, eggs, and canned salmon mixed together and made into patties equaled the most delicious treat. I would request these of my mom and if the ingredients were in the house, which they almost always were, she'd graciously oblige.

Ingredients

1 (11.75 oz.) can salmon

½ cup panko bread crumbs

1 egg, beaten

1 tsp. fresh-squeezed lemon juice

1 tsp. onion powder

½ tsp. garlic salt

Oil (enough to cover saucepan bottom)

Directions

Drain the salmon. Put the salmon in a bowl and break it up into shredded pieces with a fork. Add all the remaining ingredients except for the oil to the salmon and mix well. With hands, ball up portions of the salmon mixture and mash it into patties. The number of patties will vary based on the amount that you grab. Place the salmon patties on a plate.

Pour the oil into a frying pan or cast-iron skillet on the stovetop, and heat on medium-low. Add the salmon patties to the pan, then cook them for 5 minutes or until golden brown. Flip and repeat. Transfer the salmon patties to a paper-towel lined plate to drain off extra oil.

Serve and enjoy! This recipe can be doubled for a larger dinner meal.

Potato Salad

Potato salad is special. I don't remember a Thanksgiving without it. Although traditionally made with russet potatoes, I like to make mine with Yukon Gold potatoes. Everything else in the recipe is the traditional Southern-style potato salad.

Ingredients

4 Yukon Gold potatoes

Salt, to taste

¼ cup mayo

2 tsp. mustard

1 tsp. apple cider vinegar

1 tsp. sweet or dill relish

½ tsp. seasoning salt

Pinch of paprika

Pinch of sugar

½ celery stalk, sliced

½ cup chopped yellow or white onion

1 hard-boiled egg, chopped

Pinch of fresh dill

Directions

Peel the potatoes and cut them into cubes. Place the potatoes in a large stockpot, cover them with water, sprinkle with a bit of salt, and bring the water to a gentle boil. Boil the potatoes for approximately 10 minutes, or until just barely tender (use a fork to test tenderness). Don't overcook.

While the potatoes are boiling, mix together the salad dressing ingredients: mayo, mustard, vinegar, relish, seasoning salt, paprika, and sugar. Stir until mixed well, and set aside.

Once the potatoes are tender, strain them and rinse well with cold water. Transfer the potatoes to a mixing bowl. Stir in the celery, onion, and egg.

Add the salad dressing to the potato mixture and stir well. Add the dill and stir.

Cover the salad and refrigerate until cold, at least 3 hours.

Apple Pie

Who says we need to wait until a holiday to eat apple pie? I highly suggest you eat your apple pie warm with some whipped cream or vanilla ice cream.

Ingredients

6 to 7 large Honeycrisp apples, peeled and sliced

1 T. lemon juice

¼ cup sugar

¼ cup dark brown sugar

4 T. butter

¼ tsp. allspice

¼ tsp. cinnamon

Dash of nutmeg

1 (2 ct.) pkg. rolled, refrigerated pie crust

1 egg

1 T. water

Directions

Preheat the oven to 425°.

Place the apples in a medium bowl. Toss with the lemon juice. Add the white and dark brown sugars to the bowl and stir to coat the apples.

In a large frying pan or pot, melt the butter on medium heat. Add the apples, stir, and cook for 3 minutes. Add the allspice, cinnamon, and nutmeg. Stir. Add a lid to the pan or pot, lower the heat, and cook for approximately 10 minutes, or until apples are tender. Take off the lid and put the heat on high until the sauce is slightly carmelized and thickened. Remove from the heat.

Unroll the first pie crust onto a round 9-inch pie pan. Press slightly to fit the crust to the pan. Add the apple filling. Unroll the second pie crust and add on top of the apples. Press the edges of the 2 crusts together. If you'd like, you can use a fork to press a pattern on the edges of the crust. Slightly cut 3 slits in the top of the pie crust to allow steam to escape as the pie cooks.

In a small bowl, lightly whisk the egg with the water. Lightly brush the top of the pie crust with the egg wash.

Bake for 15 minutes at 425°. Lower the temperature to 350° and continue baking for 40 minutes more. If you notice the crust browning too quickly, cover the pie with aluminum foil and continue cooking.

Guide

Lemuel Haynes

Let all those who are strangers to the new birth be exhorted no longer to live estranged from God but labor after this holy temper of mind.[1]

One would imagine that in the late 1700s, not many would have thought that an abandoned child of a Black man and white woman, an indentured servant, would one day become one of the greatest ministers of the nineteenth century. That was Lemuel Haynes. He guided majority-white congregants to the good news of Jesus Christ and did so faithfully.

Haynes was born in West Hartford, Connecticut, on July 18, 1753. After his birth and abandonment, Haynes was an indentured servant to David Rose until 1774. He developed a deep love for theology, and the rest was history—sort of. Haynes also had an interest in politics and fought in the Revolutionary War. After that he became a minister of the gospel. Haynes is widely referred to and known as the first African American ordained minister in America.

Life and Impact

When Lemuel Haynes was an adolescent, his parents not only allegedly abandoned him, they sold him into indentured servitude. However, what man plans for evil, God plans for good. Haynes would end up in not only a Christian home but a loving home as well. From all accounts, the family treated Haynes like he was one of their own. From the investment of his new family, a godly man was born.

In many ways, the providence of God putting Haynes in that family was God's way of protecting him and likely changed the course of his entire life. Unique for that time, Haynes received an education. He was not bound to the role of servant to his family for the rest of his life. In fact, at the age of 21, Haynes was freed. Upon receiving his freedom, he enlisted and served in the Continental Army in the American Revolution. Remarkably, after the war, he returned to the home where he was an indentured servant, which would prove to be another providential move. Haynes began to write theology and his family encouraged him to pursue ministry. In 1785, Haynes became the first African American to be ordained in America.

Haynes the Guide

In order for us to truly understand how Haynes guided people toward the gospel, let's look at an excerpt from an expository teaching he wrote on John 3:3 that launched his ministry pursuit:

> To suppose that sinners can see the kingdom of God or
> be happy in the divine favor without regeneration or
> the new birth is a perfect inconsistency, or contrary
> to the nature of the thing. The very essence of religion

consists in love to God, and a man is no further happy in the favor of God than he loves God. Therefore, to say we enjoy happiness in God and at the same time hate God is a plain contradiction.[2]

In application to his sermon, he wrote:

Let all those who are strangers to the new birth be exhorted no longer to live estranged from God but labor after this holy temper of mind. Flee to Christ before it is too late. Consider that there is an aggravated condemnation that awaits all impenitent sinners. There is a day of death coming. There is a day of judgement coming. A few turns more upon the stage and we are gone. Oh, how will you answer it at the bar of God for your thus remaining enemies to him? It is sin that separates from God. But it is the being or remaining such that will eternally separate you from him. Never rest easy till you feel in you a change wrought by the Holy Spirit. And believe it—until then you are exposed to the wrath of God, and without repentance you will in a few days be lifting up your eyes in torment.[3]

Admittedly, it's hard to imagine Haynes standing before a congregation and proclaiming this sermon, let alone any sermon. During the majority of his time serving as a preacher, slavery was raging in the South. One must abandon almost all reality to envision a Black preacher sharing such bold truth to a majority-white congregation. But let's not romanticize the North. Racism and division were not isolated to the South. And although it's tough to prove, there is some suspicion that Haynes was fired from the church he served for 30 years because of his ethnic background.

What seems clear is that Haynes feared the Lord—he was so in awe of God that he didn't fear retribution for sharing the parts of God's Word that we often skirt around. A true guide doesn't tell you only what you want to hear. No, a true guide will tell you what you need to hear. For Haynes, that meant sharing the full gospel—that people are sinners in need of a Savior.

Haynes didn't only preach the gospel. He shared his thoughts about government, he opposed slavery, and he taught about a host of other topics. Here's an excerpt from his sermon "The Influence of Civil Government on Religion on Psalm 11:3":

> CIVIL government was *appointed* by God to regulate the affairs of men. Israel of old received laws, both of a civil and religious nature, from the great Legislator of the universe. This is evident to all who are acquainted with sacred or prophane history. *He removeth kings, and Jetteth up kings*, Dan. ii.21. *Thou shalt in any wise set him king over thee whom the Lord thy God shall choose*, Deut. xvii.15. St. Paul, to enforce obedience to magistracy, points to the origin of civil power, Rom, xiii. The powers that be are *ordained of God*. Whosoever, therefore, resisteth the power, resisteth the *ordinance of God*.—For he is the minister of God to thee for good. Every appointment of the Deity is favorable to religion, and conducive thereto, as there is no other object worthy [of] divine attention; to suppose otherwise would be an impious reflection on the character of God.
>
> When we consider the obvious end for which civil government was instituted, it is easy to see that it is designed as a support to virtue. To suppress vice and immorality—to defend men's lives, religion and properties, are the essential constituents of a good government.[4]

According to most accounts, Haynes was an admirer of George Washington and a Federalist. From this brief excerpt, we see that Haynes believed that the leader of a nation was called by God. It appears that his view of government is that it should care for its members and promote virtue. This seems like an idealized view of society. I would wonder if his view of a government that supports virtue fueled his criticism of a government that supported slavery.

A Faithful Proclaimer of the Gospel

As I researched Lemuel Haynes, finding writings on slavery was nearly impossible until I discovered Ruth Bogin's article in *The William and Mary Quarterly*. Dr. Bogin confirmed my perplexity:

> One of the striking facts about his prodigious output, the fruit of half a century of preaching, is its almost total silence about slavery. Two of his published speeches include tangential passages on the subject.[5]

Bogin goes on to quote Haynes's July 4 speech given in 1801. In his message he focused on liberty. He said:

> What has reduced them to their present pitiful, abject state? Is it any distinction that the God of nature hath made in their formation? Nay—but being subjected to slavery, by the cruel hands of oppressors, they have been taught to view themselves as a rank of beings far below [sic] others, which has suppressed, in a degree every principal of manhood...On the whole, does it not appear that a land of liberty is favourable to peace, happiness, virtue and religion, and should be held sacred by mankind?[6]

In the early 1980s, while doing research for a book, Bogin, a Pace University professor at the time, discovered a previously unknown document written by Haynes. The document is entitled "Liberty Further Extended" and expressed a clear, direct, and convictional argument against slavery. Haynes, as he did with everything, gave a theological argument for why slavery was unjust. The document was 46 pages long, but it was incomplete with edits that included marked-out words. After further investigation, it was determined that "Liberty Further Extended" appeared to be a draft that was meant for publication in the future.

Here's a short excerpt from his draft:

> It is not my Business to Enquire into Every particular practise, that is practised in this Land, that may come under the Odeus Character; But, what I have in view, is humbly to offer som free thoughts, on the practise of Slave-keeping. Opression, is not spoken of, nor ranked in the sacred oracles, among the Least of those sins, that are the procureing Caus of those signal Judgments, which god is pleas'd to bring upon the Children of men...

He continued:

> Every privilege that mankind Enjoy have their Origen from god; and whatever acts are passed in any Earthly Court, which are Derogatory to those Edicts that are passed in the Court of Heaven, the act is void...But, as I observed Before, those privileges that are granted to us by the Divine Being, no one has the Least right to take them from us without our consen[t].[7]

Haynes was not ashamed of the gospel. Preaching God's truth—all of it—was more important than his safety or who he was preaching to.

You and I also have the privilege of teaching our kids the good news, sharing it with our neighbors, and proclaiming it in our workplaces.

Devotion

I am not ashamed of the gospel, for it is the power of God for salvation to everyone who believes, to the Jew first and also to the Greek (Romans 1:16).

I heard the gospel for the first time at the age of 19. I may have heard it before, but it wasn't until I was a young adult that I truly understood it. Three more years would go by before I would submit my life to the Lord. At the age of 22, I walked into the church of the girl who shared the gospel with me a few years earlier, and my life was forever changed.

I often wonder what my life would have been like if the young girl had been too intimidated by me to share about Jesus and my need for Him. I was older than she was. I was a different ethnicity (she was white, I am Black). I was leading the camp where we met. She was my assistant. There were a number of reasons why she might have shied away from sharing about Christ with me. As I got to know the girl, I grew to understand her motivation: the gospel! My friend, like Lemuel Haynes, was not ashamed of the gospel. She wasn't concerned about our differences. Her motivation was that she wanted all people to know the Lord.

The apostle Paul had every reason to be ashamed of his love for the Lord and desire for others to know Him. He was once a persecutor of the church. He was a leader among the Jews. But after his radical conversion, his passion would lead Him to preach the gospel and shepherd churches to the ends of the earth. What if Paul had heard the good news and then kept it to himself? What if he had been too ashamed to submit his life to the Lord?

Paul wasn't ashamed of the gospel. Instead, he proclaimed it. With all that we know about Haynes, he, too, was more concerned that people would know the One who has the power to save. You and I also have the privilege of teaching our kids the good news, sharing it with our neighbors, and proclaiming it in our workspaces.

Discussion Questions

1. What part of Lemuel Haynes's story surprised, challenged, or inspired you?

2. Can you define *providence*? How do you see it in Lemuel Haynes's life?

3. How do you see God's providence in your life?

4. When you think of the word *guide*, what comes to mind? How was Lemuel Haynes a guide for his time? How might he still be a guide today?

5. In what situations or circumstances do you find it hard to share the gospel (e.g., at school, at work, with family members, etc.)?

6. Why shouldn't we be ashamed of the gospel?

7. **KIDS' CORNER:** What is the gospel? Why do you think pastor Lemuel Hayes wanted to tell people about Jesus?

Prayer

Pray that you would be able to recognize the kindness and faithfulness of God evident throughout your life. Ask God to help you share the gospel with others.

Ruby Bridges

Kneeling at the side of the bed and talking to the Lord made everything okay. My mother and our pastor always said you have to pray for your enemies and people who do you wrong, and that's what I did.[1]

To be the first person to do anything can be daunting. But for Ruby Bridges, it was historical, breathtaking, and heartbreaking. At six years old, Bridges would become the first African American person to integrate schools in the recently desegregated South. The landmark case and subsequent decision in *Brown v. Board of Education*—which happened to occur the same year as Bridges's birth—would change the face of American education and would forever mark the life of Ruby Bridges. The US Supreme court declared that segregation in the educational system was unconstitutional, essentially requiring schools to integrate. On November 14, 1960—six years after *Brown v. Board of Education*—Bridges took the long walk into an all-white public elementary school.

Life and Impact

Bridges was born on September 8, 1954, in the segregated and deeply racist state of Mississippi. In a 1998 *New York Times* article, Kevin Sack reported:

> After a 21-year court fight, the state of Mississippi today unsealed more than 124,000 pages of secret files from a state agency that used spy tactics, intimidation, false imprisonment, jury tampering and other illegal methods to thwart the activities of civil rights workers during the 1950s, 60s and early 70s.

> Like an eerie journey into a shadowy past, the files of the agency, the Mississippi State Sovereignty Commission, provided a profoundly unsettling reminder of the state's determination to maintain Jim Crow segregation, as reporters and individuals named in the commission's files began to review the computerized records.[2]

Life was similar in Louisiana, where the Bridges would move when Ruby was two.[3]

It is important to understand the environment and context in which little Ruby would one day walk the road toward desegregation. For the adults, it was a terrifying time. But as we'll see soon, Bridges was a child with a sweet spirit, innocence, and naivety that likely protected her and enabled her to take that road.

Brown v. Board of Education passed on May 17, 1954, and ended the 60-year reign of the Supreme Court's earlier "separate but equal" decision, marking the end of segregation. The ruling declared that the state-authorized segregation of public schools violated the 14th Amendment and was unconstitutional.[4]

Unsurprisingly for that time in our history, the Southern states were slow to integrate.

Bridges the Guide

Ruby Bridges spent her kindergarten year in a segregated school in New Orleans, Louisiana. In 1960, Bridges, along with six other children, passed a test to see if they could integrate into white schools. Although our focus is on Bridges, it's worth noting (and researching on your own) that three other young Black students integrated into an all-white school the same year as Bridges.

On the Sunday night before Bridges would walk the lonely road toward integration, Ruby's mom tried to prepare her, through tender reminders, not to fear. But Bridges was just a kid, mostly unaware of the historical significance of the journey she was embarking upon:

> All I remember thinking that night was that I wouldn't be going to school with my friends anymore, and I wasn't happy about that.[5]

On November 14, 1960, six-year-old Ruby and her mother, Lucille Bridges, were escorted into William Frantz Elementary School by four federal marshals. Through human barricades and shouts of hate, little Ruby took that long walk and changed the course of history for children in the United States. Bridges wasn't the only one to receive the wrath of a racist crowd. White families who brought their children to school also endured ridicule. But the war against integration poured well outside the schoolyard.

Bridges recalled:

> Trouble broke out across the city. As I sat quietly huddled with Mrs. Henry, mobs of protestors roamed the streets. People threw rocks and bricks at passing cars.

Some even tossed flaming bottles of gasoline. Hospital emergency rooms began to fill up.[6]

Due to the unrest and tension, Bridges was escorted to school by police for the rest of the school year. Mrs. Barbara Henry was the only teacher willing to take Ruby as a student. The two would eventually reunite during a 1996 episode of *The Oprah Winfrey Show.*

An Example of Perseverance and Prayer

Little Ruby was a young woman ahead of her time. She made the dream of Dr. Martin Luther King Jr. a possibility for children everywhere. Dr. King delivered his "I Have a Dream" speech on August 28, 1963, on the steps of the Lincoln Memorial. With power and conviction, he said,

> I have a dream that my four little children will one day live in a nation where they will not be judged by the color of their skin but by the content of their character. I have a dream today.[7]

We aren't fully there yet. But with every step toward one another, with every repenting racist, with every home opened to others, we are closer to the reality that was once a dream. When Ruby was asked how she got through those years of integration, she responded, "I really believed as a child that praying could get me through anything. I still believe that."[8] Let's learn from Ruby Bridges and be guided toward prayer.

Devotion

*Be strong and courageous. Do not fear or be in dread of
them, for it is the LORD your God who goes with you. He will
not leave you or forsake you (Deuteronomy 31:6).*

Most of us will never go into battle with a people behind a fortified city, as happened to Israel and Joshua. As they prepared to
head into the Promised Land, they were fearful, just as most of
us would have been. God reminded them that He was with them
and would never forsake them.

Although little Ruby wasn't facing a battle for land, she had
to walk through a massive sea of adults yelling, which would
have felt like going up against a fortified city. She needed great
courage, and I believe the Lord went with her. But the text
above isn't solely about Joshua's journey, Israel's fear, or little
Ruby facing racist adults. There's more: Our text reminds us of
the character of God.

The command "do not fear" is one of, if not the most, direct
orders in the Scriptures. The Lord has a lot to say about fear. God
understands that we will face circumstances that are indeed
frightening. Otherwise, there would be no reason to tell us not to
fear. Knowing that ought to bring us comfort. The Lord understands our troubles and knows we will face circumstances, situations, diagnoses, and people that will cause us to be tempted to

fear. Jesus was tempted in every way but never sinned (Hebrews 4:15). He understands.

However, God doesn't command us not to fear without providing the way out of our fear. The way out for Joshua, Israel, Ruby, and you and me is Himself. God provides Himself. He tells us, "Fear not, for I am with you; be not dismayed, for I am your God; I will strengthen you, I will help you, I will uphold you with my righteous right hand" (Isaiah 41:10). The same God who was with Israel in battle—the God who went before them and prepared a way—is the same God who is with us in our fight.

Like Ruby and Joshua, we can be courageous not because of who we are or our strength. We can be courageous because of who God is, and the good news is that He is with us.

Discussion Questions

1. What part of Ruby Bridges's story surprised, challenged, or inspired you?

2. There was one spiritual discipline that carried Bridges through. Can you identify it?

3. Ruby would not have been able to endure the school year without her teacher. Most of us will never experience anything remotely as hard and historical as being one of the first kids to integrate a school system! However, there are times when we might need to stand up for our neighbor. Have you ever experienced a situation in which you needed to lovingly support someone in a time of difficulty?

4. Do you have a situation or circumstance that requires courage right now?

5. How have you seen God help you be strong and courageous in the past? What other characteristics about God help you fight fear?

6. **KIDS' CORNER:** It would be really scary to walk into a school where no one wanted you to go. What do you think helped Ruby be brave?

Prayer

Pray for God to give you courage and strength in the face of your fears. Ask God to give you the strength and courage to stand by or stand up for someone else.

John Perkins

No amount of suffering should keep us from making sure the dignity of every human being is respected and affirmed.[1]

It's rare that we get to meet our heroes, let alone work with them. And so this brief profile feels unique and tender. As I write this, Dr. Perkins is a *living* legend. He is a humble man who would not want the fanfare. But I pray he is remembered for years and years to come. His work has helped thousands of people to understand the gospel and the gift of reconciliation: first to God and then to one another. And although it would be easy to focus on his struggles and the terrible racism he endured, I want to focus on what he would: the power of the gospel to bring unlikely people together.

Life and Impact

John Perkins was born in Mississippi in 1930 during some of the most difficult times in US history—racial segregation and the Great Depression. Similar to many at that time, Perkins endured great poverty. By the time he was one, he had already experienced tragedy when his mother died of malnutrition, leaving him to be cared for by his grandmother. By third grade, Perkins dropped out of school. In 1946, tragedy struck again when his brother, Clyde, was killed at the hands of police after he returned from fighting in World War II. Devastated, Perkins fled to California.

While in California, Perkins began advocating for social justice by forming workers into a union. In 1951, Perkins experienced two major life events. He married Vera Mae Buckley, then was drafted into the Korean War and served for three years. Although the war surely shaped him, his union with Vera has spanned a lifetime. As of 2023, the two have been married for 72 years.

Perkins became a Christian in 1957 and a Baptist minister only one year later. He moved back to his roots in Mississippi and, as a minister of the gospel, he used his love for neighbor and ministry to start Mendenhall Ministries. Through the ministry, Perkins started a day-care center, church, youth program, health center, cooperative farm, and more.[2] Remarkably, with the help of his family and the grace of God, Perkins accomplished all these initiatives in a short 12 years.

During Christmas of 1969, while many people were beginning to put up their Christmas trees and celebrate the coming of Jesus, John Perkins became the leader of the Mendenhall boycott. White retailers in the city prospered from the business of Black customers yet refused to hire Blacks, and this boycott was carried out during the Christmas season, when it would hurt the most. In 1970, while in Brandon jail, John tried to bail out several students who were unlawfully targeted and arrested by the Mississippi Highway Patrol. Perkins remained in jail and was brutally beaten for hours until his wife, Vera Mae, could bail him out. The beating was so severe that Perkins had a heart attack. He also had to have most of his stomach removed due to ulcers. After this horrific incident, the Perkins family moved to Jackson, Mississippi, where he mentored students at Tougaloo College and Jackson State University.

Perkins has lived a long life and had a fruitful ministry. In 1976, he chronicled his experiences through his first book, *Let Justice Roll Down*. The book not only told his story but shared the remarkable faith and grace he displayed in the midst of injustice and suffering. His love of neighbor, deep faith, compassion, and conviction of the power of the gospel led him to doors many would not attempt to open. From meeting with former KKK members to becoming an advisor to presidents, Perkins has lived a full life of service and sacrifice.

Perkins the Guide

Sometimes a guide will help us know how to do the right thing even when it's hard. Hebrews 11 lists several guides in the Old Testament who help us understand how to walk by faith and not by sight. When I think of John Perkins's faith in the midst of struggles, I believe he would be listed as one of the faithful who trusted God in confusing and often terrifying times and walked out his faith for all to see and benefit from.

One area of his faith that has been magnified in his life and work is his ability to forgive those who wronged him. In his book *One Blood*, Perkins wrote:

Forgiveness is the linchpin of reconciliation. It is the soil in which reconciliation takes root and grows. Forgiveness shines the brightest against the stark contrast of the darkest of tragedies. We have seen this truth at work in recent history.[3]

He continued:

To forgive is to make a decision to cancel a debt that you are owed and not to hold it against your offender. There is no forgiveness without a debt. And when we realize the enormity of our own debt it makes forgiveness possible. So in this sense forgiveness is closely connected to gratitude. If our hearts overflow with gratitude for all that the Lord has done for us, all that He did to secure our salvation, all that He continues to do to keep us—then forgiveness will be easier.[4]

A Heart for Forgiveness and Unity

Although forgiveness wasn't Perkins's only emphasis, it appears that without it, one would not be able to reconcile and enjoy the unity and love that he believes is available to us through the gospel message. The trouble with forgiveness is that it is often one-sided. It is a burden that seems unfair to bear. And that is one reason it points to Christ—the One who forgives the unforgiveable. Ultimately, it was the gospel that motivated Perkins to preach a message of unity and love:

For too long, many in the Church have argued that unity in the body of Christ across ethnic and class lines is a separate issue from the gospel. There has been the suggestion that we can be reconciled to God without being reconciled to our brothers and sisters in Christ. Scripture doesn't bear that out.[5]

Through a message of hope and a life well lived, John Perkins is an exceptional guide for all who seek to grow in their understanding of unity, love, reconciliation, and the gospel for all nations.

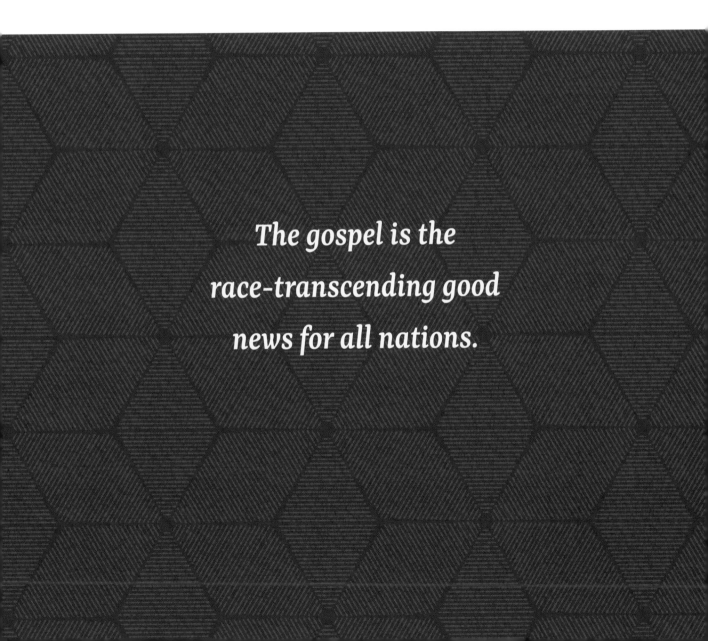

The gospel is the race-transcending good news for all nations.

Devotion

*He himself is our peace, who has made us both one
and has broken down in his flesh the dividing wall of
hostility by abolishing the law of commandments expressed
in ordinances, that he might create in himself one new man
in place of the two, so making peace, and might reconcile us
both to God in one body through the cross, thereby killing
the hostility (Ephesians 2:14-16).*

In today's culture, unity seems like an elusive goal and almost fool-ish desire. Is it really possible for people—with all their varying desires, convictions, and views—to be united in the Lord? As the saying goes, "There's nothing new under the sun." The world has felt the sting of division since Genesis 3, when sin came into the world.

In Ephesians 2:11, Paul reminded the Christians in Ephesus that at one time they were Gentiles, called "the uncircumcision." They were separated from Christ. They were alienated, strang-ers to the covenants of promise.

This was significant. The Jews despised the Gentiles; they were enemies. Jews were the covenant people of God. Being sep-arated from God is enough, but the Gentiles were also separated from God's people. They were alienated from one another. The wall of hostility was both culturally and literally in the temple building itself. One study Bible notes: "There was an inscription on the wall of the outer courtyard of the Jerusalem temple warning Gentiles that they would only have themselves to blame for their death if they passed beyond it into the inner courts."[6] The divide was deep and serious, which makes Paul's words in Ephesians 2 all the more astonishing.

The Gentiles Paul was writing to were far off. We, too, were far off—we read about it in the beginning of the chapter in Ephesians 2. We were far away from God. If you and I place our faith in the Lord, we will be saved (Ephesians 2:8-10).

As for walls of hostility, right now, you can likely think of several walls built in this century that divided and still divide nations. And there are also invisible walls—those caused by racism, racial bias, partiality, pride, arrogance, envy, and hate. These walls keep us from one another. Sometimes these walls can make it easy for us to despair. There have been many days when I have wondered if some Christians have ever read the verses about reconciliation in Ephesians 2.

Paul reminds us that we who were once far off have now been brought near by the blood of Christ. If we understand the gospel to be true—that we were indeed once far off—then we should be eager to draw near to one another.

In Ephesians 2:14, we see that the dividing wall of hostility has been abolished. We are a new people brought together by the blood of Christ. Through him we all have access to the Father. Christ has created one new man: the Christian man. Some have even called us one new race of people.

To the first-century church, this would be preposterous and miraculous. Those who were once so opposed to one another now share in the same inheritance. They are family. They may have wondered, *How could that be?* The Bible says we are no longer strangers but fellow citizens. And we aren't only fellow citizens, we are brothers and sisters in Christ.

The gospel is the race-transcending good news for all nations. It creates a new man. It's the message of Ephesians 2 and what Dr. John Perkins has based his entire ministry on. We are already created uniquely by God as image bearers, and through Christ, God abolishes the hostility. What an awesome God!

Discussion Questions

1. What part of John Perkins's story surprised, challenged, or inspired you?

2. Perkins emphasized the need for each of us to forgive one another. What were some of his reasonings?

3. Are there matters or issues in our life that keep us from loving our neighbor? Jesus helps us to forgive, and He also helps us to repent and turn from our former ways.

4. What are some ways that the gospel unites us?

5. What are some reasons that we don't experience the unity already bought for us? And how might the unity of Christians powerfully affect the world?

6. **KIDS' CORNER:** Because Jesus forgives us, we can forgive other people. Jesus also helps us to say we're sorry when we've done something wrong or unkind. How does Jesus help us?

Prayer

Ask the Lord to help you recognize times when you have struggled to forgive someone, and ask Him for the strength to forgive.

Recipes

MEAL 7

Jambalaya. 144

Corn Cakes. 147

MEAL 8

Jerk Chicken 148

Sautéed Brussels
    Sprouts 151

Rice (no recipe)

DESSERT:

Easy Semi-Homemade
    Pineapple Upside-Down
    Cake 152

Almond (Minus the Nut)
    Fudge 153

Jambalaya

Enjoy this South Louisiana dish made of fresh vegetables and delish sausage and shrimp (the shrimp is optional, but I highly recommend it).

Ingredients

2 (6 oz.) boxes long-grain rice

2 slices bacon, chopped

1½ cups chopped onion

1 cup chopped yellow pepper

½ cup chopped orange pepper

1 lb. andouille sausage

½ cup diced ham

4 cloves garlic, minced

3 cups chicken broth

1½ cups diced cooked chicken

1 (12 oz.) can diced tomatoes

2 bay leaves

½ tsp. smoked paprika

½ lb. uncooked and peeled shrimp (optional)

Directions

Preheat the oven to 400°.

Cook the rice according to the package directions and set it aside.

Cook the bacon in a large stockpot or Dutch oven. Once the bacon is browned, add the onions and peppers, cooking them until the onions are translucent. Add the sausage, ham, and garlic. Cook the mixture for 5 minutes, stirring it regularly. Add the final ingredients minus the rice. Stir and bring the mixture to a boil. Lower the temperature and pour in the rice, stirring it to blend the ingredients thoroughly.

If using a stockpot, transfer the mixture to a baking dish. If using a Dutch oven, place it directly in the oven and cover. Cook for 30 minutes and serve.

Corn Cakes

It is recorded that slaves did not have much in the way of dessert. However, for a meal with corn bread, they might have enjoyed it with molasses or honey. Our corn bread this week is perfect warm with butter and honey.

Ingredients

1 cup yellow cornmeal

1 tsp. baking powder

1 tsp. sugar

Pinch of salt

1 large egg, beaten

1 cup heavy whipping cream

Nonstick cooking spray (optional)

2 T. oil

Directions

Mix the dry ingredients together in a large bowl. Set aside.

Lightly whisk the egg and heavy cream in a small bowl. Pour the wet ingredients in with the dry ingredients and whisk until mixed.

Prepare a frying pan with nonstick cooking spray (if needed). Add the oil to the pan and warm on medium-low heat. Using a ½-cup measuring cup, scoop the corn mix into the frying pan. Cook as many cakes at a time as will fit in your pan without touching, and work in batches if needed. Cook each cake until the underside is golden brown, then flip and repeat.

Place the cooked corn cakes on a plate. Enjoy!

Jerk Chicken

"Jerk" was a method of cooking by the Maroons, escaped slaves that settled in the mountains of Jamaica. Later, this method of making tough meat tender and delicious became a seasoning.

Ingredients

2 T. of good Jamaican store-bought jerk seasoning

2 T. oil

6 chicken thighs*

6 chicken legs

Directions

Mix the seasoning and oil. Add the chicken to a bowl with a lid or a heavy-duty freezer bag. Pour the seasoning blend onto the chicken and rub until the chicken is completely covered. Refrigerate the seasoned chicken for up to 24 hours.

Preheat the oven to 400°.

Line a baking pan with aluminum foil. Spray nonstick cooking spray on the aluminum foil. Remove the chicken from the fridge. Place the chicken on the pan and put the pan in the oven. Don't overstuff (e.g. no layers) but it's okay if they touch.

Cook the chicken for 35 to 40 minutes.

Take out and serve!

*You can also use white meat if you prefer.

Sautéed Brussels Sprouts

Brussels sprouts are an easy and nutritious addition to any meal.

Ingredients

½ to 1 lb. brussels sprouts

Olive oil

2 T. chicken broth

1 clove garlic, minced

Salt and pepper to taste

Directions

Rinse the brussels sprouts and slice them in half. Add a drizzle of olive oil to a frying pan over medium heat. Add the chicken broth, then the brussels sprouts. Cook for 10 minutes, or until a light char is on the brussels sprouts. Add the garlic and continue to cook until the brussels sprouts are at the desired tenderness. If the broth evaporates and you desire softer vegetables, add another tablespoon of broth. Once the brussels sprouts have reached the proper tenderness, sprinkle them with salt and pepper. Serve.

Easy Semi-Homemade Pineapple Upside-Down Cake

I'm beginning to sound like a broken record, but it's true, not a few months went by when I was a young person that our family didn't eat pineapple upside-down cake. It was a staple. When I was in the seventh grade, I went around to area companies near my home and sold these cakes to office workers. Yes, I had a small baking business. It didn't last because I didn't understand that I had to save the money to purchase more supplies.

Ingredients

1 pkg. vanilla cake mix, plus eggs, oil, and water, according to cake mix instructions

3 T. butter

½ cup brown sugar

1 (20 oz.) can pineapple rings, drained

1 jar maraschino cherries, drained

Directions

Preheat the oven according to the cake mix directions. I use a Simple Mills Almond Flour cake mix and an 8-inch round pan. Mix the cake according to the package directions and set the batter aside.

Spray the pan with nonstick cooking spray. Add the butter to the pan and melt it in the oven. Remove the pan from the oven and sprinkle the brown sugar across the surface of the melted butter. Add the pineapple rings to the pan, spacing them evenly in a single layer. You are unlikely to use the whole can of pineapples. Add a cherry to the center of each pineapple ring, placing additional cherries in the empty spaces in the pan. Pour the batter evenly over the pineapples. Bake until the top is lightly browned or until a toothpick inserted in the center comes out clean.

Allow the cake to cool. Using a platter or cake plate, turn the pineapple upside-down cake over and remove the pan, so that the pineapples are on top.

Enjoy!

Almond (Minus the Nut) Fudge

Every Christmas, my mom would make a large batch of chocolate fudge. It remains a treat for us to indulge in as many pieces as humanly possible when mom decides to make some. My mom added vanilla extract, but to add a twist (and because I love almond flavoring), enjoy this almond fudge. Feel free to add a cup of *real* nuts if you prefer.

Ingredients

1½ sticks butter

3 cups sugar

⅔ cup evaporated milk

2 cups semisweet chocolate morsels

7 oz. marshmallow cream

2 tsp. almond extract

Directions

Lightly grease an 8 × 8-inch pan.

Put the butter, sugar, and milk in a heavy pot over medium-low heat, stirring until the butter is melted and the mixture is smooth. Raise the heat slightly, stirring constantly until the mixture begins to boil. Continue stirring and boil for 5 minutes, or until the sugar is fully dissolved (if you have a candy thermometer, cook until the mixture reaches 250°).

Remove the pot from the heat. Add the chocolate morsels and stir until fully melted. Add the marshmallow cream and almond extract and stir until fully incorporated. Pour the fudge into the greased pan.

Refrigerate for at least two hours to set. This fudge is delicious frozen as well.

Messenger

Phillis Wheatley

And O that when my flesh and my heart fail me God would be my strength and portion for ever, that I might put my whole trust and Confidence in him, who has promis'd never to forsake those who Seek him with the whole heart.[1]

Writers often write from their experience, and for Phillis Wheatley, that meant writing from the deep pain and sorrow of being torn from her homeland in Africa, experiencing a treacherous journey across the Atlantic Ocean, and landing in a foreign place to be sold into slavery. John Wheatley bought her and named her after the ship that brought her to America. Wheatley had a unique experience for slaves, including an education and support from her owners to learn how to write. Wheatley began writing poetry around the age of 13 years old.

Life and Impact

We don't know Phillis Wheatley's exact date of birth, but we do know that she was forced out of Africa and experienced the dreadful Middle Passage, the name given to describe the voyage of enslaved Africans traveling across the Atlantic in slave ships. The trip took an estimated 240 days. She landed in Boston, Massachusetts, and in July 1761, was bought by John Wheatley as a gift to his wife, Susanna.[2] We don't know what Phillis's name was before she landed and was sold. Likely an unexpected providence, her name was given to her as a slave but would one day be worth $253,000.[3]

Wheatley began writing letters at a young age, and her first may have been written in 1765, at the age of 12. She was given the opportunity to study English, classical literature, poetry, geography, history, Latin, the Bible, and other Christian texts.[4] Wheatley's first published poem appeared in the *Newport Mercury* newspaper on December 21, 1767. It is believed that Susanna Wheatley helped secure the publication and would help secure others in the future. Because we don't know Phillis's exact date of birth, it is hard to say definitively that her first letter was written at the age of 12, because that would mean her first published work would have appeared at the age of 13 or 14. By the time she was a teenager, Phillis had experienced a lot of life and was wise beyond her years. Her poetry, including the poem published in 1767, often included Christian themes.

In 1771, Wheatley's recognition and popularity grew exponentially. She wrote an elegy that was published publicly in London as well as in Boston. Her elegy was addressed to Selina Hastings, Countess of Huntington, about the death of her chaplain, George Whitefield. Wheatley went on to publish poems in *The London Magazine* and more.

Susanna Wheatley attempted to publish a book of Phillis Wheatley's poems in Boston, but that effort failed. She then looked to London for a publisher. Archibald Bell agreed to publish Wheatley's book *Poems on Various Subjects, Religious and Moral*, to be released in 1773. Wheatley traveled to England and hoped to be there for six weeks, but was only there for approximately ten days because Susanna became ill. She returned to Boston to nurse Susanna back to health.

Although it is not recorded whether Wheatley returned joyfully out of love for her mistress or was forced to go, I believe the incident proves that the appearance of freedom does not mean true freedom and agency. She was indeed still indentured to the Wheatley family. Biographer Vincent Carretta asserts that she may have negotiated her freedom by accompanying Susanna back to Boston.[5] Carretta wondered if Wheatley had heard about the liberation of slaves while she was in England and suggested that may have given her the courage to advocate for her own freedom. He surmised that Wheatley was likely influenced by her meetings with the British abolitionist Granville Sharp, whom she spent quite a bit of time with during her visit to England.[6]

The Messenger

Wheatley returned to America on September 13, 1773, and was freed by October 18. She received her first copies of her book of poems in January 1774. It wasn't until after she was no longer enslaved that she began to write more freely about her opposition to slavery.

One example of her anti-slavery writing can be found in a letter to Mary Wooster, titled, "On the Death of General Wooster":

> For ever grateful let them live to thee
> And keep them ever Virtuous, brave, and free—

But how, presumtuous shall we hope to find

Divine acceptance with th' Almighty mind—

While yet (O deed Ungenerous!) they disgrace

And hold in bondage Afric's blameless race?

Let Virtue reign—And thou accord our prayers

Be victory our's, and generous freedom theirs.[7]

There has been some criticism (or perhaps confusion) about some of Phillis's writings. For example, she wrote a poem titled "On Being Brought from Africa to America," which, on the first read, seems to glorify America even though she endured slavery there.

'Twas mercy brought me from my *Pagan* land,

Taught my benighted soul to understand

That there's a God, that there's a *Saviour* too;

Once I redemption neither sought nor knew.

Some view our sable race with scornful eye,

"Their colour is a diabolic die."

Remember, *Christians*, *Negros*, black as *Cain*,

May be refin'd, and join th' angelic train.[8]

There's a part of me that wonders if she was expressing artistic sarcasm because of what she wrote in a similar vein in a poem titled "To the Right Honourable William, Earl of Dartmouth":

Should you, my lord, while you peruse my song,

Wonder from whence my love of *Freedom* sprung,

Whence flow these wishes for the common good,

By feeling hearts alone best understood,

I, young in life, by seeming cruel fate

Was snatch'd from *Afric's* fancy'd happy seat:

What pangs excruciating must molest,

What sorrow labour in my parent's breast?

Steel'd was that soul and by no misery mov'd

That from a father seiz'd his babe belov'd:

Such, such my case. And can I then but pray

Others may never feel tyrannic sway?[9]

Susanna Wheatley died on March 3, 1774. Interestingly, Phillis was invited to join other African-born people to become a missionary to Africa, for which she declined.[10] By 1778, John Wheatley and his son Nathaniel Wheatley had died. Phillis then married John Peters, lost all her children in infancy, and suffered extreme poverty.

Her Words Live On

By most (if not all) accounts, Wheatley was like family to her owners. Slaves, when helped, seem free, but they are still slaves. It could be easy to read some of their stories and assume an easier life, but we get only part of the story—the part that survived history. For Phillis, once the support of the Wheatley family ended due to their deaths, she struggled to sell her work, and it is believed that she never published again. Sadly, if Wheatley had stayed in England, where she was adored and honored, there is a chance that she would have continued to publish. When the Wheatley family died, Phillis's story went dark in more ways than one, until her death in 1784.[11] Her story may have died, but her writings live on.

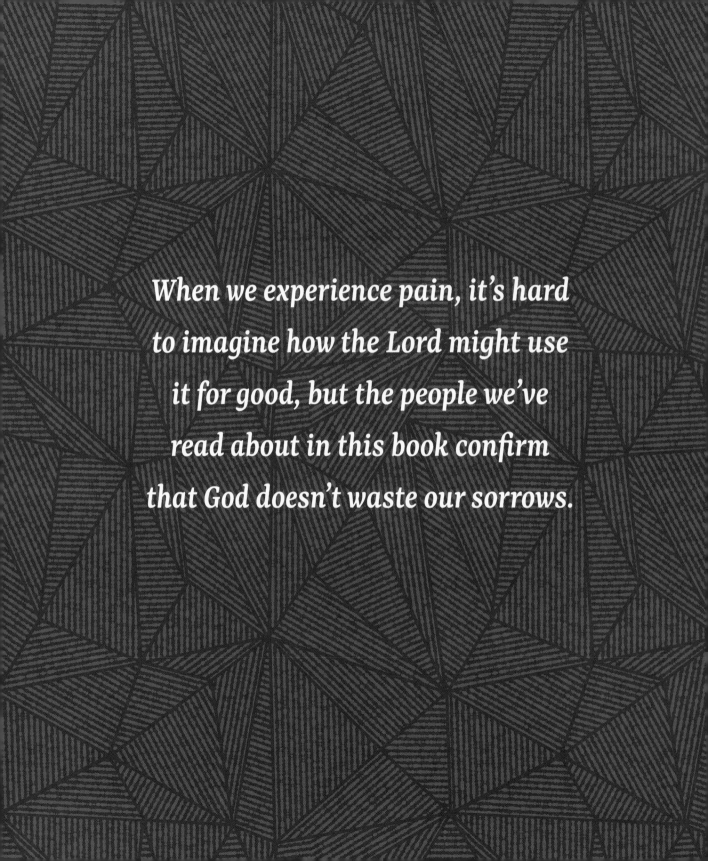

When we experience pain, it's hard to imagine how the Lord might use it for good, but the people we've read about in this book confirm that God doesn't waste our sorrows.

Devotion

Blessed be the God and Father of our Lord Jesus Christ, the Father of mercies and God of all comfort, who comforts us in all our affliction, so that we may be able to comfort those who are in any affliction, with the comfort with which we ourselves are comforted by God (2 Corinthians 1:3-4).

If we live long enough, we will experience suffering. It may not be in the form of a dreadful disease or terminal diagnosis, but we can be certain that we will suffer. In our world, we experience pain of all kinds. Sometimes there's not much we can do about our pain, but when someone else who has suffered in the same way comes alongside us and cares for us, their comfort can mean a lot to us.

When I think about all the people and stories that I've featured in *Celebrating Around the Table*, I think of this text in 2 Corinthians. Each of the individuals we've met on these pages experienced deep suffering. Their challenges could have led to self-loathing and withdrawal. Who would have blamed them? They've collectively experienced slavery, discrimination, poverty, fear, and so much more. But each one of them turned their suffering into actions that were helpful for others. In the case of Wheatley, she turned her pain into the written word to comfort others. When we experience pain, it's hard to imagine how the

Lord might use it for good, but the people we've read about in this book confirm that God doesn't waste our sorrows.

I remember a particular season when I needed God's comfort. I had experienced a great loss and was dreadfully sad. The Lord reminded me, through His Word, that He draws near to the brokenhearted and will never leave nor forsake them (Psalm 34:18; Deuteronomy 31:8). The Lord comforted me. He helped me to see that I was not alone and that I could pray to Him in my distress. Then, one day it happened—a person experienced a similar loss, and I was able to comfort them with the comfort I had received from Christ.

We can't always make sense of what is happening in our lives, and in the midst of hard circumstances, it can be tough to see how God might use the situation or our pain, especially for the good of others. But He can and He will. There's a saying that comes to mind—I don't know where it came from, but it goes something like, "When you are lifted up, turn around and lift someone else." With the words I saw a picture of someone on top of a hill, reaching down to pull up another person. The reference is likely about achievement and not suffering, but I believe the concept fits with what we're learning here. All the people featured in this book could have used their achievements to serve themselves only. They did not. They took their pain and sorrow and turned it into action, service, preaching, and poetry.

Discussion Questions

1. What part of Phillis Wheatley's story surprised, challenged, or inspired you?

2. What helpful messages can you find in the short excerpts of Wheatley's writing above?

3. Have you ever used art, writing, music, photography, or other forms of artistic expression to share a message? Consider this message: Scripture says God is the God of all comfort. Using that as a prompt, write something (anything) for five minutes, and then share your words with the others around you (or a friend later).

4. Have you ever experienced someone comforting you? How did it make you feel?

5. Name one hard situation you've experienced. How has God comforted you in it, and how might He be preparing you to comfort others who face a similar situation?

6. **KIDS' CORNER:** When you are sad, what makes you feel better? Whenever we are sad, God will help us. And sometimes He will use our parents, friends, or siblings to help us too.

Prayer

If you are experiencing pain or sorrow, cry out to the Lord and ask Him to draw near to you and comfort you. If you know someone else who is experiencing suffering or pain, pray for that person.

Sojourner Truth

I feel safe in the midst of my enemies, for the truth is all powerful and will prevail.[1]

Sojourner Truth was born Isabella Baumfree in 1797 in Ulster County, New York. Truth was enslaved with her parents until she was nine, when she was sold to another home. She was sold several times after and endured harsh treatment, suffering in unimaginable ways. Her testimony of hope and trust in Jesus are compelling and inspiring, but her story ought to cause lament. Her life illustrates the devastating effects of slavery. Yet it also magnifies the power of a relationship with Jesus.

Life and Impact

Sojourner Truth's family was torn apart due to slavery. Her parents, James and Betsey, took great care of their children while they were with them. Devastatingly, each child was sold away. Truth found her mom crying and inquired as to why, and her mom said, "Oh, my child, I am thinking of your brothers and sisters that have been sold away from me."[2] Truth didn't know how many brothers and sisters she had, but there were at least eight, likely more. Truth would experience the same destructive assault on her own family later in life.

As a child, Truth remembered living in a cellar underneath a hotel. The slaves slept on the damp floor, on top of straw like animals. A biographer, Olive Gilbert, lamented,

Still, she does not attribute this cruelty—for cruelty it certainly is, to be so unmindful of the health and comfort of any being, leaving entirely out of sight his more important part, his everlasting interest—so much to any innate or constitutional cruelty of the master, as to that gigantic inconsistency, that inherited habit among slave-holders, of expecting a willing and intelligent obedience from the slave, because he is a MAN—at the same time every thing belonging to the soul-harrowing system does its best to crush the last vestage of a man within him; and when it *is* crushed, and often before, he is denied the comforts of life, on the plea that he knows neither the want nor the use of them, and because he is considered to be a little more or a little *less* than a beast.[3]

The Messenger

Many years later, in 1851, at a woman's rights convention in Akron, Ohio, in her famous speech "Ain't I a Woman?," Truth is said to have cried out, *"I have borne thirteen children, and seen most all sold off to slavery, and when I cried out with my mother's grief, none but Jesus heard me! And ain't I a woman?"*[4]

Slavery ended in New York state in 1827, and Truth's owner had promised that she would be freed one year ahead of the time. When the time came for her freedom, he refused to honor that promise, and she ran away. In retaliation, the slave owner sold one of her sons into slavery in Alabama, where slavery was still legal. She sued him and won her case. Her son was returned to her.

Sojourner Truth's life took various turns after that. She lived with a Quaker family, then eventually moved and settled in New York City. After some time, she found a church to attend, called Mother African Methodist Episcopal Zion Church. It wasn't until 1843 that she left New York City and moved to Northampton, Massachusetts, where she met two important abolitionists.

While living in a commune, Truth met the brother of William Lloyd Garrison, who was an abolitionist, journalist, and the owner and editor of the anti-slavery newspaper *The Liberator*. She also met Frederick Douglass, and from then onward became a leading voice for the abolition of slavery. Her life story, *The Narrative of Sojourner Truth*, was published by *The Liberator* in 1850, written by her biographer, Olive Gilbert. Sojourner Truth was illiterate, but that did not stop her from using her voice.

The historical accounts of Truth's life vary, but they include tales of her shouting at Frederick Douglass as he despaired over whether slavery would end: "Frederick, is God dead?"[5] Meaning,

God *isn't* dead and has the power to end slavery. What faith! By all accounts, Truth did have faith, and it was her faith that helped empower her voice.

Harriet Beecher Stowe wrote an article about Sojourner Truth titled "Libyan Sibyl," which appeared in the April 1863 issue of *The Atlantic Monthly* and is still available to read at *The Atlantic*. Here, Truth recounted her testimony, which was part of her talks as she went around preaching the gospel to anyone who would listen:

> Pretty well don't need no help; an' I gin up prayin.' I lived there two or three years, an' then the slaves in New York were all set free, an' ole massa came to our home to make a visit, an' he asked me ef I didn't want to go back an' see the folks on the ole place. An' I told him I did. So he said, ef I'd jes' git into the wagon with him, he'd carry me over. Well, jest as I was goin' out to git into the wagon, *I met God!* An' says I, "O God, I didn't know as you was so great!" An' I turned right round an' come into the house, an' set down in my room; for 't was God all around me. I could feel it burnin', burnin', burnin' all around me, an' goin' through me; an' I saw I was so wicked, it seemed as ef it would burn me up. An' I said, "O somebody, somebody, stand between God an' me! for it burns me!" Then, honey, when I said so, I felt as it were somethin' like an *amberill* [umbrella] that came between me an' the light, an' I felt it was *somebody*—somebody that stood between me an' God; an' it felt cool, like a shade; an' says I, "Who's this that stands between me an' God? Is it old Cato?" He was a pious old preacher; but then I seemed to see Cato in the light, an' he was all polluted an' vile, like me; an' I said, "Is it old Sally?"

an' then I saw her, an' she seemed jes' so. An' then says I, "*Who* is this?" An' then, honey, for a while it was like the sun shinin' in a pail o' water, when it moves up an' down; for I begun to feel 't was somebody that loved me; an' I tried to know him. An' I said, "I know you! I know you! I know you!"—an" then I said, "I don't know you! I don't know you! I don't know you!" An' when I said, "I know you, I know you," the light came; an' when I said, "I don't know you, I don't know you," it went, jes' like the sun in a pail o' water. An' finally somethin' spoke out in me an' said, "*This is Jesus!*" An' I spoke out with all my might, an' says I, "*This is Jesus!* Glory be to God!" An' then the whole world grew bright, an' the trees they waved an' waved in glory, an' every little bit o' stone on the ground shone like glass; an' I shouted an' said, "Praise, praise, praise to the Lord!" An' I begun to feel such a love in my soul as I never felt before—love to all creatures. An' then, all of a sudden, it stopped, an' I said, "Dar's de white folks, that have abused you an' beat you an' abused your people—think o' them!" But then there came another rush of love through my soul, an' I cried out loud, "Lord, Lord, I can love *even de white folks!*"[6]

A Heart for Forgiveness

That last line stuck out to me. In my profile on John Perkins, I shared how forgiveness can often be one-sided. Here we see the same conviction from Sojourner Truth. In her book *Caste*, Isabel Wilkerson quotes an essayist and author who wrote after the Charleston church massacre in 2015, "Black people forgive because we need to survive...We have to forgive time and time again while racism or white silence in the face of racism continues to thrive. We have had to forgive slavery, segregation..."[7] I cannot speak for the essayist, but clearly, we cannot say that all white people are silent about injustice and racism. But when they are, it is often the burden of the Black brother or sister to extend forgiveness.

The need to forgive to survive seems to ring true in almost every ex-slave, abolitionist, and civil rights leader's account that I read. Not that everyone forgave; I haven't read enough to account for that. But so many of them had faith and applied their faith in the way they viewed their oppressor, even if it meant that they were the only ones obeying the Lord's command to forgive. In other words, those who endured suffering at the hands of others often had to move forward without any real acknowledgment from the one who wronged them. There was a dignity in their extension of forgiveness—a humanity that I wish had been extended in return to these great Black men and women. God knows and remembers.

Truth's power and message lived on well past her death. She died in Battle Creek, Michigan, on November 26, 1883, at the age of 86. Her eulogy was delivered by Frederick Douglass.

Devotion

We are his workmanship, created in Christ Jesus for good works, which God prepared beforehand, that we should walk in them (Ephesians 2:10).

I was dead, and by God's grace, God brought me to Himself. I'm not talking about physical death, obviously. I'm talking about spiritual death, which is true of all of us until salvation in Christ. I became a Christian at the age of 22 after a young girl shared the gospel with me. The girl and I couldn't have been more different from one another. God sent her aflame for Jesus and His gospel to share the good news with me.

I remember one of the first times I read Ephesians 2. The reality that my salvation is a free gift still overwhelms me to this day. By a free gift, I was made alive by grace through faith (verses 1-10). I love the book of Ephesians, and specifically these verses. There's no question that it takes the power of our triune God to change our hearts of stone into hearts of flesh.

So, when I read about the radical transformation of Isabella Baumfree, I can't help but think about the radical power of the gospel in my own life. After her conversion to Christianity, Isabella named herself Sojourner Truth. She named herself

Sojourner because she decided she would travel to share her testimony and help people see their sin. She named herself Truth because she would declare God's truth to the people she encountered.[8] The message of the gospel will lead people to do radical things for the Lord and for others. And Truth's sacrificial love and powerful voice likely changed the lives of generations of people.

Sojourner Truth could never have known the good work the Lord had in store for her life. Similarly, we don't know what the Lord has for us to do in the future. But we do know this from Ephesians 2:10: "We are his workmanship, created in Christ Jesus for good works, which God prepared beforehand, that we should walk in them." The Lord may not call you or me thousands of miles away from our home, but whatever He does, we can know that He will go before us.

Discussion Questions

1. What part of Sojourner Truth's story surprised, challenged, or inspired you?

2. Truth's story, likely more than the other stories featured, highlights the horrible effects of slavery on African families or the families born into slavery. In what ways do you think slavery affected these families?

3. Take time to reflect on Ephesians 2:1-10. If you are with others now, share your testimony. If you are alone, write it out and reflect on when you gave your life to the Lord.

4. With Sojourner Truth's journey in mind, what good works do you believe the Lord is calling you to do this week (e.g., serve in a children's ministry, sit with a lonely person at the lunch table, etc.)?

5. Sojourner Truth used her voice to help lift up others. She did this by sharing her testimony, fighting for civil rights, and lending her voice for women's rights. What is one practical way you can help lift up others in your neighborhood, church, or community (e.g., volunteer at a women's shelter, donate to a charity, sponsor a child, etc.)?

6. **KIDS' CORNER:** We have used the word *abolitionist* several times now. It's a big word! What do you think *abolish* means? (Hint: if something has a beginning but you want it to stop or _____?) An abolitionist is someone who attempts to abolish something. What was Sojourner Truth trying to help get abolished?

Prayer

Thank the Lord that He thought of you before the foundation of the world. Ask God to help you know what to do today to love Him and serve others.

Mahalia Jackson

Gospel music is nothing but singing of good tidings—spreading the good news. It will last as long as any music because it is sung straight from the human heart.[1]

Known as the Queen of Gospel, Mahalia Jackson was a singer involved in the civil rights movement, and she sang before Martin Luther King Jr. presented his "I Have a Dream" speech on August 28, 1963. One of my greatest heroes of the faith might not be considered a theologian by typical standards, but I believe she was. Through her singing and activism, Mahalia brought sorrows to life and shined bright the glory of Jesus, our only hope. Her words and passion consistently remind me to endure in the Christian faith.

Life and Impact

Mahalia Jackson was born in New Orleans in 1911. Her grand-parents were born into slavery but freed after the Civil War. She grew up relatively poor, describing her home as a "shack" where if it rained outside, it rained in her home.[2] Her family was devoted to Christian doctrines and the church. Her Christian upbringing fueled her desire to sing gospel music. It also informed how she saw the world and lived.

In her autobiography, Jackson reflected:

> The principle of Christianity is right. If we don't apply it, it's a fault of ours, not the Lord. I would not feel deserving of what Christianity has done for me if I did all the things that some people do today. It's gotten to be that people think they have to have everything. I say you can't have it and you don't have any business doing it if you're a Christian.[3]

When Jackson was young, her uncle moved to Chicago. She remembered him telling stories of Black and white people shopping together and being in the same dressing room. To a young Mahalia who only knew strict and unrelenting Black Codes (restrictive laws to reinforce segregation and limit the freedoms of African Americans[4]) and Jim Crow laws, the stories were amazing and awe-inspiring. After listening to story after story, she began to have a longing to move to Chicago. We should note that although Chicago didn't enforce strict segregation, the state of Illinois did adopt and execute Black Codes.[5] But Chicago was a land of opportunity, and Jackson wanted to experience it.

In 1928, at the age of 16 years, Mahalia Jackson packed her things and moved from New Orleans to Chicago. She didn't have to traverse alone. Her aunt joined her on the trip, and she lived with family already there. Her move to Chicago would mark the beginning of her public music ministry.

The Messenger

In Chicago, Jackson helped form a group called the Johnson Gospel Singers. During the Great Depression, the trio group helped churches pay their mortgages through concerts. By the early 1930s, she broke off from the group to continue to sing gospel music on her own, and invitations for her to sing in local churches and conventions ramped up. In her early days, Jackson traveled with professor Thomas A. Dorsey, often regarded as the father of gospel music and himself the composer of many gospel songs, including "Take My Hand, Precious Lord" and "There'll Be Peace in the Valley for Me."[6] She valued his gifts and music and often performed these songs on stage.

But not all Christians embraced gospel music. Many Chicago-area pastors opposed it and thought it was undignified. They were concerned about the physical expressions that accompanied the music, such as clapping and stomping. For these pastors, gospel music was too close to jazz. Reflecting on a time when a pastor spoke against her from the pulpit, Jackson wrote,

> I got right up, too. I told him I was born to sing gospel music. Nobody had to teach me. I was serving God. I told him I had been reading the Bible every day most of my life and there was a Psalm that said: "Oh, clap your hands, all ye people! Shout unto the Lord with the voice of the trumpet!" If it was undignified it was what the Bible told me to do.[7]

The criticism did not stop Jackson from singing. She had a deep faith in Jesus and trusted that her music was for Him. Where others may have been discouraged and turned to more popular music and venues, she did not. Jackson didn't look down on people who did not live like her. However, she had a conviction about living a modest and humble life. She wrote:

> Another thing that gave me the strength to stay with my gospel songs is that all the high life and show business has never had any attraction for me. Maybe it's the Lord's will that makes me that way, but I've never had a longing to spend my time in fancy places or go in for high society.[8]

Jackson could control the type of music she sang, but fame came to her whether she wanted it or not. By the late 1940s and early 1950s, Jackson was a gospel-singing superstar. She began receiving invitations—some she accepted, others she did not—to large and prestigious venues such as The Apollo Theater, Carnegie Hall, and the White House.

It's fascinating reading Ms. Jackson's autobiography. Chapter by chapter, she names people she interacted with who could all easily be featured in this book! From Martin Luther King Sr. and Jr. to Rosa Parks, Jackson was extremely connected. Those connections were friends but served another purpose for the greater good. She supported and was an active member of the civil rights movement.

On August 28, 1963, Mahalia Jackson took to the stage to use her beautiful, soulful voice to encourage the souls of more than a quarter million men and women gathered at the Lincoln Memorial for the March on Washington, organized to advocate for the civil and economic rights of African Americans.

Jackson endured many trials as she got involved in the civil rights movement by singing and providing financial support. As her gospel music gained widespread popularity, she received death threats from neighbors in her quiet Chicago neighborhood.

During that day at the Lincoln Memorial, she would be instrumental in the creation of Martin Luther King Jr.'s most famous speech, "I Have a Dream." She reportedly called out from behind him on the podium, "Tell 'em about the dream, Martin. Tell 'em about the dream!" That urging led him to ditch his notes and use the refrain "I have a dream."

Devoted to Singing God's Praises

Jackson's place in history, including but not limited to gospel music and the civil rights movement, is remarkable yet not widely known. She was devoted to living out the gospel and singing God's praises. And on the day of King's "I Have a Dream" speech, she belted out two songs. The first, "How I Got Over," is a song of endurance in the face of hardship, and the lyrics describe her own hard times. How did she "get over"? She looked to Jesus, the One who died and suffered for her. She sang songs of praise to her Savior, thanking Him for how He protected and provided for her. She knew the Lord would never leave nor forsake her, and she proclaimed it through song.

Even with all her fame and notoriety, Jackson never forgot her roots. She exuded humility and grace:

> Ever since I began singing in the big concert halls, people have been trying to teach me to be grand, but I just can't do it. Some folks get so grand that you can't hand them a letter from home, but I just know how they can get that way. If blessings come to you, accept them, but don't let them dominate you.[9]

Mahalia Jackson's steadfastness and convictions are a reminder and message to all of us to stay the course, remember the gospel, and entrust our lives and work to the Lord.

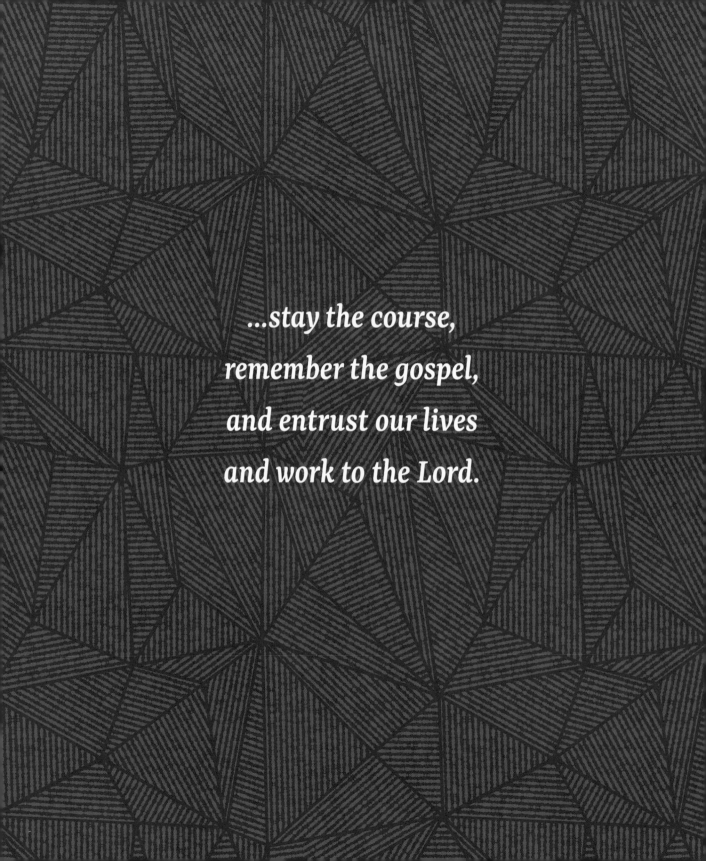

...stay the course,
remember the gospel,
and entrust our lives
and work to the Lord.

Devotion

Do not be slothful in zeal, be fervent in spirit, serve the Lord. Rejoice in hope, be patient in tribulation, be constant in prayer (Romans 12:11-12).

In Romans 12, the apostle Paul helps Christians to understand what it looks like to follow Jesus. Some Bible translations label the section "Marks of the True Christian." When I think of someone who emulates these attributes, I think of Paul himself. Here's how he describes the suffering he endured:

> Five times I received at the hands of the Jews the forty lashes less one. Three times I was beaten with rods. Once I was stoned. Three times I was shipwrecked; a night and a day I was adrift at sea; on frequent journeys, in danger from rivers, danger from robbers, danger from my own people, danger from Gentiles, danger in the city, danger in the wilderness, danger at sea, danger from false brothers; in toil and hardship, through many a sleepless night, in hunger and thirst, often without food, in cold and exposure. And, apart from other things, there is the daily pressure on me of my anxiety for all the churches. Who is weak, and I am not weak? Who is made to fall, and I am not indignant (2 Corinthians 11:24-29)?

Paul endured extreme hardship. Yet throughout his letters to churches, he wrote about hope, perseverance, faith, and serving the Lord and others. He lived out the calling to be patient in tribulation. And from all that we know about Mahalia Jackson, it would appear that she, too, embodied these characteristics.

Jackson did not become slothful in her zeal and passion for the Lord. She fervently served God with her gifts. She was patient in troubling times and sufferings. She had a desire to serve the Lord with her voice. She rejoiced with great hope in the Lord and helped others rejoice too. And although we don't know if she was fervent in prayer, we do know that she was fervent in praise.

These characteristics aren't reserved for the so-called "super Christian." Paul was writing to ordinary believers like you and me. And although the stories of people like Mahalia Jackson are remarkable, they were also ordinary Christians serving an extraordinary God. None of us can grow apart from Jesus (John 15:5). Therefore, if we want to grow in being zealous for the Lord, faithful in prayer, and patient in trials, you and I must lean on the Lord's grace and strength. We can't do anything on our own. God will help us grow; we need only to ask Him for His help (John 15:7).

Discussion Questions

1. What part of Mahalia Jackson's story surprised, challenged, or inspired you?

2. Gospel music has been a staple in our church culture for so long that it's hard to imagine it was once frowned upon. Is there anything we can learn about how Jackson responded to the criticism she experienced and how that might translate to us today?

3. Has music played a part in your discipleship journey? If yes, how? If not, how could it benefit you?

4. What are some specific ways you can apply Romans 12:11-12? For example, you could plan a time during which you read God's Word and write out your prayers in response to the Lord.

5. With a group or as an individual, take a moment to search for your favorite gospel song, hymn, or worship song and sing it or carefully read it and interpret the lyrics in your own words.

6. **KIDS' CORNER:** Write down five things you are thankful for and say a prayer thanking God for them. For example, if you write, "I am thankful for my family," you can pray, "Thank You, Lord, for my family. I love them so much. You are so kind to give them to me, God. Amen."

Prayer

Ask the Lord to restore or rejuvenate your passion for Him. Ask Him to help you grow in your prayer life and to lean on Him during trials. Cast all your burdens onto the Lord.

Recipes

MEAL 9

Fried Chicken 188

Mashed Potatoes 191

Sautéed Green Beans 192

MEAL 10

Shrimp and Grits 194

Salad (no recipe)

DESSERT:

Banana Pudding 196

Sweet Potato Pie 197

Fried Chicken

Who doesn't enjoy some good ole fried chicken? It was a staple in my home growing up. Although I don't cook it (or eat it) as much as I did when I was young, when I do, my heart and taste buds are very happy. This Southern staple is a hit.

Ingredients

1 whole chicken, cut into pieces
6 additional chicken legs or thighs
   (optional)
Garlic salt
3 cups buttermilk
   (enough to cover chicken)
2 cups flour

1 T. salt
1 tsp. pepper
1 tsp. garlic powder
1 tsp. onion powder
½ tsp. cayenne pepper
1 to 1½ cups canola oil

Directions

Place the chicken pieces on a baking sheet and sprinkle them all over with garlic salt. Add the seasoned chicken to a large bowl with a lid. Pour in the buttermilk, adding more buttermilk as needed until the chicken is fully covered. Cover the bowl and refrigerate the chicken at least 4 hours.

Preheat the oven to 350°.

Add the flour to a freezer bag (or any sealable bag). Add the salt, pepper, garlic, onion, and cayenne pepper. Shake the bag to mix.

Pour off the buttermilk. Add two pieces of the chicken to the bag, seal it, and then shake to thoroughly coat the chicken. Add the flour-coated chicken to a foil-lined baking sheet. Repeat this process with all the chicken pieces.

Add the canola oil to a frying pan or cast-iron skillet and turn the heat to medium-low. Add 1 cup of oil. If the oil is too shallow, add an additional ½ cup. Add the chicken to the frying pan, being careful to leave space for flipping. Let the chicken cook for 15 minutes, or until it is golden brown, then flip each piece. Cook the chicken for 15 more minutes. Once the chicken is golden brown, add it to a new baking dish lined with aluminum foil. Place the chicken in the oven and bake it for 30 minutes.

Remove the chicken from the oven and serve.

Mashed Potatoes

My mom used russet potatoes, but I love the smooth taste of Yukon Golds. You can use the potato you prefer. I make these potatoes to taste. So I'll give you a starting place, but add more butter, cream, salt, and pepper as desired.

Ingredients

8 Yukon Gold potatoes, peeled and
   cut into chunks
2 tsp. salt

4 T. butter
½ cup heavy cream
Salt and pepper, to taste

Directions

Add the potatoes to a large stockpot and cover with water. Add the salt. Cover the pot and bring the water to a boil, boiling until the potatoes are tender. Turn off the heat. Drain the potatoes, then return them to the pot. Add the butter, and mash the potatoes with the butter using a hand masher. Add the heavy cream and mix thoroughly. Add salt and pepper to taste.

If using a stand mixer, add the boiled potatoes, butter, and cream and mix until fully incorporated. Add salt and pepper to taste, then stir.

Serve immediately.

Sautéed Green Beans

I grew up eating soft but not mushy vegetables, so I prefer my green beans very soft. If you prefer softer green beans, try the Boiled Green Beans on page 62. But I also love sautéed green beans and believe these pair perfectly with any meal. Enjoy!

Ingredients

1 lb. green beans, trimmed and cut

2 T. chicken broth

1 T. olive oil

½ onion, sliced

1 garlic clove, minced

1 tsp. garlic salt

Directions

Add the green beans, broth, and olive oil to a large frying pan and sauté over medium heat for 5 minutes. Add the onions, garlic, and salt. Cook until the onions are translucent or soft, stirring frequently. If needed, add additional broth or oil a teaspoon at a time.

Serve and enjoy!

Shrimp and Grits

The history of shrimp and grits will depend on who you are talking to and what you are reading. We know that slaves used grits. The use of grits remained in the South and was passed down for generations. I ate grits almost every morning (butter and sugar!—if you know, you know). Almost every source will note that grits originated with Native Americans before making its way to enslaved Africans. Today, it's on almost every Southern menu and a staple in towns such as Charleston, South Carolina.

Ingredients

For the grits

1 cup stone-ground grits
2½ cups water
1½ cups heavy whipping cream
2 T. butter

1 tsp. salt
Pinch of pepper
1 to 1½ cups shredded mild cheddar cheese

For the shrimp

6 slices bacon, chopped
1 T. olive oil
1 lb. peeled, deveined uncooked shrimp (approximately 26 to 30)
1 tsp. Cajun seasoning
1 red bell pepper, chopped

4 green onions, chopped
4 cloves garlic, minced
⅓ cup chicken broth
1 tsp. Worcestershire sauce
1 lemon (2 tsp. lemon juice)

Directions

Prepare the grits: Place the grits, water, heavy cream, butter, salt, and pepper in a pot. Stir. Bring the mixture to a boil. Lower the heat to a simmer and cook for 30 minutes. (If you use instant grits, follow the package instructions, then add the butter and cream and stir.) Once the grits are finished, stir in 1 cup of cheese and turn off the heat. For a cheesier grit, add an additional ½ cup of cheese.

While the grits cook, add the bacon to a large frying pan. Fry the bacon pieces until they are golden brown and cooked through. Transfer the bacon to a plate. Add the olive oil to the same pan, adjusting the burner to medium heat. Add the shrimp to the pan in a single layer. Sprinkle the Cajun seasoning on the shrimp and sear for 1 to 2 minutes, or until the flesh of the shrimp turns pink. Flip the shrimp and repeat. You may desire more seasoning (I do!) so feel free to sprinkle with additional cajun seasoning. Place the shrimp on a plate and set aside.

Add more oil to the frying pan if needed, then add the red peppers and cook them until slightly tender (about 5 minutes). Add the green onions and garlic. Cook for 2 minutes. Add the broth, Worcestershire sauce, and lemon juice, then stir. Then add the shrimp and bacon. Adjust the heat to low and stir. Take off heat once finished and set aside as you assemble your dish.

Serve immediately. Here's how I serve this dish: Taste the grits and add additional salt and pepper if needed. Add a serving of the grits to a bowl and then top with a scoop of the shrimp mixture.

Banana Pudding

I have a confession. Banana pudding isn't my favorite dessert. I'd even say that I don't like it much. But it's a staple and I would have been disappointed in myself had I not included it. I changed the recipe and now I love it! I've added two ingredients (heavy cream and cream cheese) that I hope might help other banana pudding skeptics enjoy it more too!

Ingredients

2 cups heavy whipping cream

2 cups cold milk

2 (3.4 oz.) pkgs. instant vanilla pudding

1 tsp. vanilla extract

1 (14 oz.) can sweetened condensed milk

1 (8 oz.) pkg. cream cheese, softened

4 cups vanilla wafers

5 bananas, sliced

Premade whipped cream* (optional)

*You've already made homemade whipped cream! You can repeat the whipped cream portion of this recipe using only 1 cup of heavy whipping cream. Once the cream is whipped, fold in two tablespoons of powdered sugar.

Directions

Add the heavy whipping cream to the bowl of an electric mixer. Blend on medium, leaving it mixing until the liquid becomes thick and fluffy. If you'd prefer to use a hand mixer, blend on medium until you achieve the same result. Reserve the whipped cream in a bowl. Fill a larger bowl with ice. Nestle the bowl of whipped cream into the ice bowl to chill. Set aside.

Add the milk, pudding mixes, and vanilla to a mixing bowl and blend the mixture until thick. Mix in the sweetened condensed milk and cream cheese, blending it until fully incorporated. Fold in the chilled whipped cream.

Grab a serving dish of choice. Glass dishes make a nice presentation. You can use a trifle dish and layer it three times or an 8 × 8-inch pan and layer it twice.

Add a single layer of wafers, then a layer of sliced bananas. Spread a portion of the pudding on top of the sliced bananas. Repeat the layering process, being sure to end with pudding as the final layer. Garnish with whipped cream.

Sweet Potato Pie

During the autumn season, we see an onslaught of pumpkin-flavored items. From drinks to specialty candies, pumpkin is having its day. Pumpkin pie is also a favorite for many. However, I did not grow up on pumpkin. Sweet potato pie was always at the cookout and on the Thanksgiving menu!

Ingredients

2 large eggs

¾ cup dark brown sugar

1 (8 oz.) pkg. cream cheese, at room temperature

4 T. melted butter

3 cups sweet potato puree, or 2 (15 oz.) cans

1 T. vanilla

1 tsp. ginger

1 tsp. nutmeg

½ tsp. cinnamon

½ tsp. cloves

1 (9-inch) deep-dish pie crust in tin (favorite brand, thawed if frozen)

Directions

Preheat the oven to 350°.

Add the eggs and sugar to a mixing bowl and mix for one minute using any kind of electric mixer. Add the cream cheese and butter to the sugar blend and mix until incorporated. Add the sweet potato and blend for 1 minute. Add the vanilla and spices, then blend well.

Using a fork, poke a few small holes across the bottom of the pie crust. Spread the sweet potato mixture in the pie crust. Place the pie on a cookie sheet, then bake for 60 minutes or until set (you may need to cook this longer). Test the pie for doneness by shaking it slightly to see if there's a slight jiggle in the center. If there's a jiggle just in the center, it's ready.

Cool the pie for at least 30 minutes before serving.

Continuing to Celebrate

You've made it all the way to this conclusion, or maybe you've skipped around and landed here. However you arrived here, I hope you are coming away with a greater knowledge and understanding about a small fraction of our shared history. I imagine that as you gathered around the table to discuss some of these stories, there were times when you didn't feel like you were celebrating. You might have lamented that John Perkins had to endure the unjust murder of his brother. You may have become righteously angry as you read about George Liele being thrown in jail to stop the spread of the gospel because it came from a Black man. Maybe you wept at the thought of Sojourner Truth's children being ripped away from her and sold into slavery. That doesn't sound like something we would celebrate, does it? Yet celebrating doesn't have to involve confetti. Here are some synonyms for *celebrate*: commend, exalt, extol, feast, and rejoice. You likely did at least one, if not all, of those things as you read along. So, thank you for celebrating around the table with me as we commended, exalted, extoled, feasted, and rejoiced in the ways God worked in other people's lives.

So, what are some next steps you can take? Here are a few suggestions:

1. I highly recommend that you look through my endnotes and find the biographies or books I quoted from—books that you can read so you can learn more. I shared a lot, but gave you only a small taste of what's available. The full stories of every one of these people are rich and meaningful.

2. Search for other African American people to study about and learn from.

3. Apply this idea and concept to other cultures and people groups. My family is very intentional about studying a variety of people. Doing this will encourage growth, understanding, and love. It's also a lot of fun!

4. As you read this book, were you convicted in certain areas of your life? Ask the Lord to give you the grace to change and look to God's Word for guidance and instruction.

It has been a privilege to share with you through *Celebrating Around the Table*, and I'm so glad for the opportunity to share my family's tradition with you.

With gratefulness,

Trillia

Notes

WEEK ONE FREEDOM

Frederick Douglass

1 "[Introduction]," *Counterpoints* 406 (2012): 1. http://www.jstor.org/stable/42981613.

2 Frederick Douglass, *Narrative of the Life of Frederick Douglass* (Boston, MA: Anti-Slavery Office, 1845), 11.

3 Frederick Douglass, *My Bondage and My Freedom* (Digireads.com Publishing, 2011), Location 740.

4 Douglass, *Narrative of the Life of Frederick Douglass*, 34.

5 Douglass, *Narrative of the Life of Frederick Douglass*, 93.

6 "Biographies: Frederick Douglass," *PBS*, https://www.pbs.org/blackpress/news_bios/douglass.html.

7 "Douglas Portraits," *American Writers Museum*, https://exhibits.americanwritersmuseum.org/exhibits/frederick-douglass/portraits/.

8 Melissa Lindberg, "Frederick Douglass and the Power of Pictures," *Library of Congress Blogs*, February 28, 2020, https://blogs.loc.gov/picturethis/2020/02/frederick-douglass-and-the-power-of-pictures/.

9 F.J. Grimké, "The Second Marriage of Frederick Douglass," *The Journal of Negro History* 19, no. 3 (1934): 324-329.

10 A version of this introduction was first published as: Trillia Newbell, "Introduction," in *Narrative of the Life of Frederick Douglass*, (Trinity Forum, 2020), https://www.ttf.org/product/frederickdouglass/.

Elizabeth Freeman

1 Gloria J. Browne-Marshall, "1619 to 1819: Tell Them We Fought Back, A Socio-Legal Perspective." *Phylon* 57, no. 1 (2020): 49. https://www.jstor.org/stable/26924986.

2 Ben Z. Rose, *Mother of Freedom: Mumbet and the Roots of Abolition* (Lincoln, MA: Treeline Press, 2020), 12.

3 "Massachusetts Constitution and the Abolition of Slavery," *Mass.gov*, https://www.mass.gov/guides/massachusetts-constitution-and-the-abolition-of-slavery.

4 "The tombstone of Elizabeth Freeman (Mum Bett)", *PBS*, http://www.pbs.org/wgbh/aia/part2/2h36t.html.

Harriet Tubman

1 "Quotes," Harriet Tubman Historical Society, http://www.harriet -tubman.org/quotes/.

2 When researching Harriet Tubman, you will find that the numbers range from 70 to 700. Historians have settled that it is more likely to be around 70 individuals. Barbara Maranzani, "Harriet Tubman: 8 Facts About the Daring Abolitionist," *History.com.* January 4, 2023, last modified, https://www.history .com/news/harriet-tubman-facts-daring-raid; https://www .nps.gov/hatu/planyourvisit/upload/MD_TubmanFactSheet _MythsFacts_2.pdf.

3 Sarah H. Bradford, *Harriet Tubman: The Moses of Her People* (Digireads.com Publishing), 11.

4 Bradford, *Harriet Tubman*, 11

5 Bradford, *Harriet Tubman*, 11.

6 Bradford, *Harriet Tubman*, 8.

7 Minty Ross was married to John Tubman in 1844. She took his name, but he seems to be a minor part of her story. However, she did return to try to get him, but he had already remarried. She took her vows seriously and did not remarry until his death. Kelly Hancock, "Printing the Legend: The Unseen Courage of Harriet Tubman," *The American Civil War Museum*, February 19, 2021, https://acwm.org/blog/printing-the-legend-the-unseen -courage-of-harriet-tubman/.

8 Catherine Clinton, *Harriet Tubman: The Road to Freedom* (Boston, MA: Little, Brown, and Company, 2004), 39-40.

9 Bradford, *Harriet Tubman*, 15.

10 "Harriet Tubman's Boston: c. 1858", *National Park Service*, https:// www.nps.gov/articles/000/htubman-boston-c1858.htm#_ftn6.

11 Kate Clifford Larson, *Bound for the Promised Land: Harriet Tubman, Portrait of an American Hero* (New York: One World Ballantine Books, 2004), 175-177.

12 A version of this first appeared in the Bible study by Trillia J. Newbell, *A Great Cloud of Witnesses* (Chicago, IL: Moody Publishers, 2021), 72-74.

13 Ben Shive, Andrew Peterson, "Is He Worthy?" *Resurrection Letters, Vol. 1* (Nashville, TN: Centricity Music, 2018), https://www .azlyrics.com/lyrics/andrewpeterson/isheworthy.html.

Betsey Stockton

1   Betsey Stockton, as cited in *The Christian Advocate, Vol. III* (Philadelphia: A. Finley, 1825), 39.

2   Brian Johnson and Robert J. Stevens, eds., *Profiles of African-American Missionaries* (Pasadena, CA: William Carey Library, 2012), 144.

3   John A. Andrew, "Betsey Stockton: Stranger in a Strange Land," *Journal of Presbyterian History (1962-1985)* 52, no. 2 (1974): 158, http://www.jstor.org/stable/23327601.

4   Betsey Stockton, as cited in *The Christian Advocate, Vol. II* (Philadelphia: A Finley, 1824), 233.

5   Betsey Stockton, as cited in *The Christian Advocate, Vol. II* (Philadelphia: A Finley, 1824), 234.

6   Betsey Stockton, as cited in *The Christian Advocate, Vol. III* (Philadelphia: A. Finley, 1825), 39.

7   Johnson and Stevens, eds., *Profiles of African-American Missionaries*, 157-159.

8   Gregory Nobles, "Betsey Stockton," *Princeton & Slavery*, https://slavery.princeton.edu/stories/betsey-stockton#ref-43.

George Liele

1   Milton C. Sernett, ed., *African American Religious History: A Documentary Witness* (Durham, NC: Duke University Press, 1999), 45-46.

2   David T. Shannon, Julia Frazier White, et al., eds., *George Liele's Life and Legacy: An Unsung Hero* (Macon, GA: Mercer University Press, 2013), 92.

3   Sernett, ed. *African American Religious History: A Documentary Witness*, 46.

4   Shannon, ed., *George Liele's Life and Legacy*, 116-117.

5   Shannon, ed., *George Liele's Life and Legacy*, 118.

6   Johnson and Stevens, eds. *Profiles of African-American Missionaries*, 32.

Charlotte L. Forten Grimké

1   Ray Allen Billington, ed., *The Journal of Charlotte L. Forten: A young black woman's reactions to the white world of the Civil War era* (New York: The Dryden Press, 1953), 109.

2   Frederick Douglass, *Life and Times of Frederick Douglass* (Oxford: Oxford University Press, 2022), 74.

3   Billington, ed., *The Journal of Charlotte L. Forten*, 46.

4   "Charlotte Forten Grimké," *National Park Service*, https://www.nps.gov/people/charlotte-forten-grimke.htm.

5   Billington, ed., *The Journal of Charlotte L. Forten*, 136-137.

6   Billington, ed., *The Journal of Charlotte L. Forten*, 145-146.

7   Billington, ed., *The Journal of Charlotte L. Forten*, 148.

8   Billington, ed., *The Journal of Charlotte L. Forten*, 150.

Lemuel Haynes

1 Lemuel Haynes, *Selected Sermons* (Wheaton, IL: Crossway, 2023), 62.

2 Haynes, *Selected Sermons*, 48-49.

3 Haynes, *Selected Sermons*, 62-63.

4 "Haynes, Lemuel," *Evans Early American Imprint Collection*, https://quod.lib.umich.edu/e/evans/N25513.0001.001?view=toc.

5 Ruth Bogin, "'Liberty Further Extended': A 1776 Antislavery Manuscript by Lemuel Haynes," *The William and Mary Quarterly* 40, no. 1 (1983): 88, https://doi.org/10.2307/1919529.

6 Bogin, "'Liberty Further Extended': A 1776 Antislavery Manuscript by Lemuel Haynes."

7 Bogin, "'Liberty Further Extended': A 1776 Antislavery Manuscript by Lemuel Haynes."

Ruby Bridges

1 Ruby Bridges, *Through My Eyes* (New York: Scholastic Press, 1999), 48.

2 Kevin Sack, "Mississippi Reveals Dark Secrets of a Racist Time," *The New York Times*, March 18, 1998, https://www.nytimes.com/1998/03/18/us/mississippi-reveals-dark-secrets-of-a-racist-time.html.

3 Lauren Ewen Blokker, "The African American Experience in Louisiana," https://www.crt.state.la.us/Assets/OCD/hp/nationalregister/historic_contexts/The_African_American_Experience_in_Louisiana.pdf.

4 "Plessy v. Ferguson (1896)", *National Archives*, https://www.archives.gov/milestone-documents/plessy-v-ferguson.

5 Bridges, *Through My Eyes*, 14.

6 Bridges, *Through My Eyes*, 32.

7 Martin Luther King Jr., "I Have a Dream," https://www.npr.org/2010/01/18/122701268/i-have-a-dream-speech-in-its-entirety.

8 Bridges, *Through My Eyes*, 56.

John Perkins

1 John M. Perkins, *Count It All Joy* (Chicago, IL: Moody Publishers, 2021), 89.

2 "The Life of John M. Perkins," *johnmperkins.com*, https://www.johnmperkins.com/#:~:text=In%2012%20years%2C%20John%20Perkins,and%20an%20adult%20education%20program.

3 John M. Perkins, *One Blood* (Chicago, IL: Moody Publishers, 2018), 99.

4 Perkins, *One Blood*, 102.

5 Perkins, *One Blood*, 32.

6 ESV Study Bible (Wheaton, IL: Crossway Books, 2008), 2265.

Phillis Wheatley

1 Vincent Carretta, ed., *Complete Writings: Phillis Wheatley* (New York: Penguin, 2001), 141.
2 Vincent Carretta, *Phillis Wheatley: Biography of a Genius in Bondage* (Athens, GA: University of Georgia Press, 2011), 1.
3 In 2005, one of Wheatley's letters sold at auction for $253,000. Vincent Carretta, *Phillis Wheatley*, ix.
4 Carretta, ed., *Complete Writings*, xvi.
5 Carretta, ed., *Complete Writings*, xxvii.
6 Carretta, ed., *Complete Writings*, xxvi.
7 Carretta, ed., *Complete Writings*, 93.
8 Carretta, ed., *Complete Writings*, 13.
9 Carretta, ed., *Complete Writings*, 40.
10 Carretta, ed., *Complete Writings*, xxxiii.
11 Carretta, *Phillis Wheatley*, 196.

Sojourner Truth

1 Neil Irvin Painter, *Narrative of Sojourner Truth* (New York: Penguin, 1998), 96.
2 Painter, *Narrative of Sojourner Truth*, 11.
3 Painter, *Narrative of Sojourner Truth*, 10.
4 I took the liberty to modernize the language because all texts written about Truth's speech are from sources writing her words rather than from her pen. The direct quote is, "I have borne thirteen chillen, and seen 'em mos' all sold off into slavery, and when I cried out with a mother's grief, none but Jesus heard—and ar'n't I a woman?" Sojourner Truth, "Speech to Woman's Rights Convention," in Ted Widmer, ed., *American Speeches: Political Oratory from the Revolution to the Civil War* (New York: The Library of America, 2006), 524.
5 Marvin A. McMickle, ed., *An Encyclopedia of African American Christian Heritage* (Valley Forge, PA: Judson Press, 1972), 166.
6 Harriet Beecher Stowe, "Sojourner Truth, The Libyan Sibyl," *The Atlantic Monthly*, April 1863, https://www.theatlantic.com/magazine/archive/1863/04/sojourner-truth-the-libyan-sibyl/308775/.
7 Isabel Wilkerson, *Caste: The Origins of Our Discontents* (New York: Random House, 2020), 288.
8 "Sojourner Truth," *African American Odyssey*, https://www.loc.gov/exhibits/odyssey/educate/truth.

Mahalia Jackson

1 Mahalia Jackson, *Movin' On Up* (New York: Hawthorn Books, 1966), 12.
2 Jackson, *Movin' On Up*, 12.
3 Jackson, *Movin' On Up*, 20.
4 "Black Codes," History, last modifed March 29, 2023, https://www.history.com/topics/black-history/black-codes.
5 Mark Wyman and John W. Muirhead, "Jim Crow Comes to Central Illinois: Racial Segregation in Twentieth-Century Bloomington-Normal," *Journal of the Illinois State Historical Society* 110, no. 2 (July 1, 2017): 154-182, https://doi.org/10.5406/jillistathistsoc.110.2.0154.
6 "Thomas A. Dorsey," *Songwriters Hall of Fame*, https://www.songhall.org/awards/winner/Thomas_A_Dorsey.
7 Jackson, *Movin' On Up*, 63.
8 Jackson, *Movin' On Up*, 68.
9 Jackson, *Movin' On Up*, 11.

Recipe Index

Apple Pie *110*

Banana Pudding *196*

Beef Stew *56*

Black Eyed Peas *100*

Brussels Sprouts (Sautéed) *151*

Butter (Homemade) *60, 105*

Chicken (Fried) *188*

Chicken (Jerk) *148*

Chicken and Stuffing (One-Dish) *61*

Corn Bread *59, 104*

Corn Cakes *147*

Fudge (Almond) *153*

Green Beans (Boiled) *62*

Green Beans (Sautéed) *192*

Greens *103*

Jambalaya *144*

Mac and Cheese (Creamy) *107*

Meat Loaf *63*

Pineapple Upside-Down Cake
  (Easy Semi-Homemade) *152*

Potato Salad *109*

Potatoes (Mashed) *191*

Red Velvet Cake with Cream Cheese Icing *65*

Ribs (Baked) *106*

Roasted Root Vegetables *64*

Salmon Croquettes *108*

Shrimp and Grits *194*

Sweet Potato Pie *197*

About
the Author

Trillia J. Newbell is a bestselling author whose many books include *God's Very Good Idea*, *Fear and Faith*, and *If God Is For Us*. When she isn't writing, she is encouraging and supporting other writers as the acquisitions director at Moody Publishers. Trillia is married to her best friend, Thern, and they reside with their two children near Nashville, Tennessee.